The Economics of Public Health

Heather Brown

The Economics of Public Health

Evaluating Public Health Interventions

Heather Brown
Newcastle University
Newcastle upon Tyne, UK

ISBN 978-3-319-74825-2   ISBN 978-3-319-74826-9   (eBook)
https://doi.org/10.1007/978-3-319-74826-9

Library of Congress Control Number: 2018936518

Cover pattern © Harvey Loake

Printed on acid-free paper

This Palgrave Pivot imprint is published by the registered company Springer International Publishing AG part of Springer Nature
The registered company address is: Gewerbestrasse 11, 6330 Cham, Switzerland

Preface

This book introduces students to a wide range of techniques from main-stream economics and health economics that can be applied to the evaluation of public health policy and public health issues. To aid understanding and help students apply theory in practice, the book includes a large number of empirical examples. These are from developed countries and will show the reader how economic tools can be applied to public health. Where applicable, cross-country comparisons are used to illustrate how contextual factors related to health care systems, demographics, and environmental factors may impact on outcomes and the cost-effectiveness of public health policies.

This book is divided into three main sections. It begins with an introduction to public health economics and indicates how economics can contribute to the development of public health policy. The second section outlines how observational data can be used for policy evaluation and discusses potential datasets that can be used for analysis. The final section outlines different estimation techniques and their strengths and weaknesses, providing examples of when they are appropriate. The book finishes with a checklist for evaluating public health policy by using observational data.

The book is targeted at public health professionals who have some experience with the implementation of public health policy but may not have the experience or toolkits to undertake an economic evaluation of these policies. Higher level economic undergraduate students who have some previous experience of econometrics, economic evaluation techniques, and microeconometric theory will find this book a useful addition to their toolkit. Postgraduate economic students wishing to understand how economic theory can be applied to the real world will also find this book useful.

Newcastle upon Tyne, UK   Heather Brown

Contents

List of Figures

List of Tables

Part I

Introduction

1

Introduction to Public Health Economics

Learning Outcomes:

- Distinguish between micro- and macroeconomics
- Give an example of technical and allocative efficiency
- Identify the four main types of economic evaluation
- Define public health economics

Why Do We Need Economics in Public Health?

Non-communicable diseases have surpassed infectious diseases as the leading cause of morbidity and mortality in developed countries. Prevention and treatment of the causes and consequences of lifestyle-related diseases will form an important part of health policy in the twenty-first century. Resources are limited, so we cannot purchase or produce everything that we would like to have. Economics is the study of this scarcity and how we deal with it. There are two main areas in economics. *Microeconomics* focuses on the decisions taken by individuals, households, and firms, and the way that they contribute to the setting of prices

© The Author(s) 2018
H. Brown, *The Economics of Public Health*,
https://doi.org/10.1007/978-3-319-74826-9_1

and outputs in the market. *Macroeconomics* focuses on the interaction of broad aggregates and interaction between different sectors of the economy.

How then does this relate to public health and the health sector? Most treatment options available exceed the budgets of individuals, insurance systems, and governments to pay for everything. A choice needs to be made about which treatments should be purchased and what policy should be enacted. One way in which this choice can be made is by prioritising alternative treatments and policies through an analysis of their cost and benefits.

Health Economics focuses on obtaining the maximum value for money by ensuring that not just the treatments with clinical effectiveness but those that are cost-effective are funded. The basic task of any health economic evaluation is to:

* Identify
* Measure
* Value

the costs and consequences of the alternatives being considered.

* *Identify*: Without systematic analysis it is difficult to identify clearly the relevant alternatives. For example, in deciding to introduce a new screening programme for breast cancer survivors it is necessary to describe existing activities (i.e. annual general practitioner (GP) check-ups) as an alternative programme to which new proposals must be compared.
* *Measure*: What outcomes are we concerned with: life years extended, health improvement, number of cases detected, for example. How can we quantify these outcomes?
* *Value*: Without the measurement and comparison of outputs and inputs we have little upon which to base value for money. The real cost of any programme is not the cost appearing on the programme budget but rather the health outcome achievable in some other programmes which have been foregone by committing resources to the chosen programme.

Health economic evaluation is used to address questions of *technical* and *allocative* efficiency. Technical efficiency relates to the relationship between resources related to capital and labour and health outcomes. An intervention is technically efficient if the same (or better) outcome could NOT be produced with less of one type of input (either capital or labour). An example of a question addressing technical efficiency is:

'What is the most efficient way of providing dialysis for patients with chronic renal failure—hospital based or at the patient's home?'

- The question addresses a particular condition (chronic renal failure).
- There is a fixed resource (existing budget for treating chronic renal failure).

The question relates to *how* to best use the given set of resources for kidney dialysis.

Allocative efficiency takes account of how resources are distributed within the community. It also takes account of the productive efficiency for which health care resources are used to produce health outcomes. The societal perspective of allocative efficiency is rooted in welfare economics. It is achieved when resources are allocated so as to maximise the welfare of the community. An example of a question relating to allocative efficiency is:

'Should we expand the provision of hospital haemodialysis or introduce a screening programme for prostate cancer in men aged over 55 years?'

- The question relates to two different conditions (chronic renal failure vs prostate cancer).
- There is a proposed change in how resources are used.

The question relates to *what* intervention is the best use of resources across the entire government budget.

In all economic evaluations, the final result is presented as a ratio of *incremental cost* and *effects (outcomes)*.

- Incremental refers to a change in costs for a change in benefits/effects/ outcomes.

Table 1.1 Four main types of economic evaluation

Type of evaluation	Comparison and outcomes	Common unit of measurement of outcome
Cost-minimisation analysis	Single effect of interest common to both alternatives. Outcomes are identical	Money
Cost-effectiveness analysis (CEA)	Single effect of interest common to both alternatives, but achieved to different degrees.	– Life years gained – Pain reduction – Cases detected
Cost-utility analysis (CUA)	Single or multiple effects, not necessarily common to both alternatives.	– Quality Adjusted Life Years (QALYs) (generic or condition-specific) – Healthy Life Years Extended (HYEs)
Cost-benefit analysis (CBA)	Single or multiple effects, not necessarily common to both alternatives.	Money, e.g. – Human capital – Willingness to pay

- Cost is in the numerator (top half of fraction).
- Effects or Outcome are in the denominator (bottom half of fraction).
- Costs are always expressed in monetary terms.

How effects are expressed depends on the type of evaluation you are doing. There are four main types of economic evaluation, which are presented in Table 1.1.

What Makes Public Health Different from the Production of Televisions?

Markets are institutions that bring together buyers and sellers of goods and services. There are two main types of market: *free markets*, where there is little to no intervention by the government except to enforce contracts or the private ownership of property; and *regulated markets*, where government directly regulates how goods, services, and labour may be priced, used, and distributed. This is related to how competitive a market is. Market competition is based upon how many firms are willing and able to sell a good or service and how easy it is for firms to enter or exit the market in the long run. Market competition is usually classified as either *perfect competition, oligopoly,* or *monopoly.* Perfect competition is thought of as the gold standard of market types, as it results in an efficient allocation of resources since firms cannot manipulate prices and there is perfect information regarding prices for both consumers and producers. Firms in an oligopoly market and a monopoly market can manipulate price and the number of goods supplied, which can reduce consumer surplus.

Compared with, say, the market for televisions, where there is less of a case for government regulation of the market, even in countries with a relatively lax view towards regulation of markets such as the USA, the market for health care is still regulated. This is because of a number of failures in the health care market and provision of public health in particular. There are the problems of *externalities, provision of public goods,* and *asymmetric information.*

Externalities are when the market does not account for all the costs and benefits associated with the provision of a good or service. A prime public example can be traced back to the MMR scare in the late 1990s. Wakefield et al. 1998 showed a link between the MMR vaccine and childhood autism, and this provoked a decrease in the number of parents vaccinating their children. There are public and private benefits to vaccination, and these are illustrated in Fig. 1.1.

If the critical number of children are not vaccinated there will not be herd immunity to measles, increasing the likelihood that there will be an outbreak. The economist toolkit can be used to assist policymakers and practitioners in developing policy to incentivise parents to vaccinate their children. We will return to this example in Chap. 3, when we explore how discrete choice experiments can be used to elicit parents' views on vaccination programmes and what factors influence their decisions to vaccinate their children.

A public good is a good or service that can be consumed simultaneously by everyone and that no one can be excluded from consuming. People may not want to pay for the good or service because they know that once it is provided anyone can consume it (the free rider problem). The provision of health care is not a public good, because if one person

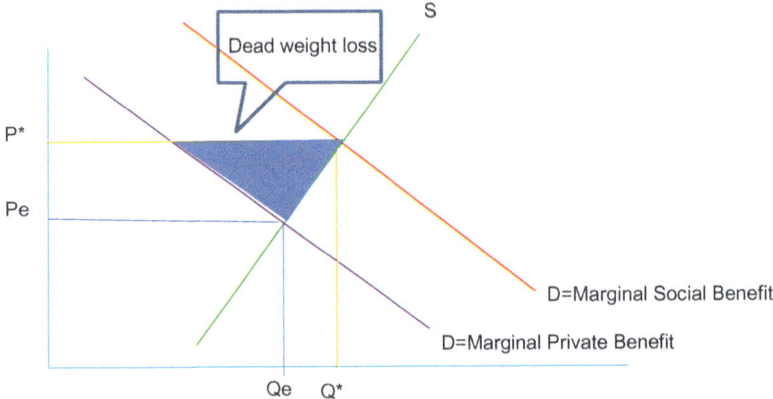

Dead weight loss is a loss of economic efficiency from sub-optimal consumption. This can be thought of as the difference between Pe and Qe (private equilibrium) instead of P* and Q* (social equilibrium).

Fig. 1.1 Private and social demand for MMR vaccine. Note: Dead weight loss is a loss of economic efficiency from sub-optimal consumption. This can be thought of as the difference between Pe and Qe (private equilibrium) instead of P* and Q* (social equilibrium)

receives treatment this excludes someone else from receiving the same treatment. However, aspects of public health can be considered public goods. An example is infection control through the management and provision of clean drinking water. Everyone can benefit from having access to clean drinking water without excluding anyone from this benefit. Information campaigns which are an integral part of public health campaigns to raise awareness of physical activity or eating fruit and vegetables can also be thought of as public goods. Everyone has access to this information, conditional on having the appropriate medium to access it, and no one can be excluded from consuming this information. Because of the universality of public goods, individuals may consume more than their fair share of the good or service. Additionally, there may be lower production than the socially optimal amount. Therefore, markets will undersupply the provision of public goods. Governments usually need to supply or finance the provision of public goods to ensure that the socially optimal amount is provided. In Chap. 3, we will explore if voluntary partnerships such as the UK government's Responsibility Deal with 21 fast food companies to promote healthy eating is effective and how we can evaluate it.

Finally, there is the problem of asymmetric information, when one party of an economic transaction has more information than the other party. The cost for the uninformed party to obtain the required information to ensure a fair transaction is prohibitively expensive. This can lead to transactions that work against the uninformed party, resulting in market failure. The provision of health care is a prime example of asymmetric information as most medical information is technically complex, coupled with the fact that many medical conditions do not repeat themselves. The cost of making a mistake in a health-related transaction is greater and less reversible than other services as a wrong choice could lead to death. It is also often difficult to postpone treatment and 'shop around' for different opinions. Governments need to regulate the market and create effective incentives to ensure that health professionals work towards patients' best interests.

What is Public Health Economics?

Traditionally, public health economics has been considered to be a sub-discipline of health economics. This has meant that the focus of public health economics has been on evaluating the efficiency of public health interventions through the use of economic evaluation techniques, as discussed above in the section 'What Makes Public Health Different from the Production of Televisions?'. Carande-Kulis et al. (2007) propose that this definition be expanded. They suggest that because of market failures such as lack of full employment (not everyone who would like to work has a job) and the inefficient provision of public goods, the full impact of consumer and producer behaviour from public health interventions are not reflected in economic evaluations.

Standard outcome measures used in health economics such as The Quality Adjust Life Year (Torrance and Feeny 1989), which is commonly estimated from the EQ-5D (Devlin et al. 2003), is a generic five-dimensional measure of health covering mobility, self-care, usual activities, pain/discomfort, and anxiety and depression. Each dimension can be measured using a three- or five-level response. For example, with the EQ-5D-5L each dimension has five levels: no problems, slight problems, moderate problems, severe problems, and extreme problems. It is possible that these dimensions are not sensitive to the outcomes that are being targeted by public health interventions. An economic evaluation will therefore be unable to determine if a policy or intervention is actually cost-effective. Partial capture of the outcomes of interest could lead policymakers and practitioners to policies that exacerbate health inequalities.

Changing behaviour or preventing the uptake of unhealthy behaviour and activities often requires different types of interventions to those used to treat other medical conditions. As many practitioners will be well aware, governments and other stakeholders sometimes decide to evaluate a public health policy after it has been implemented. Additionally, with public health policy, policymakers and practitioners occasionally require an *ex ante* analysis of a potential policy to assess if it should be implemented. Thus, evaluation techniques appropriate for use with Randomised Control Trials (RCT), the gold standard in medical evaluation (Kaptchuk 2001), may not be possible.

This means that new and innovative methodology is required to evaluate and inform the development of public health policy. This book introduces the reader to public health economics. Carande-Kulis et al. (2007) defines public health economics as the study of the economic role of government in public health, particularly but not exclusively in supplying public goods and addressing externalities. In this book, we plan upon expanding on this definition. The definition we use is: *Public health economics attempts to quantify the costs associated with lifestyle-related diseases and other public health issues. Evaluate prevention and treatment options compared with standard practice as well as to design toolkits to help the decision-making process for policymakers and health professionals, and allow them to determine if public health policies should be implemented.* Public health economics utilises a range of techniques from both mainstream economics and health economics. In this book we do not focus on quantifying the costs of public health interventions but on estimating the effects of public health interventions and policy. The methods proposed in this book therefore have a wider scope and can be used beyond those for standard economic evaluations. However, as we do not explore how to capture and estimate cost equations, we do not focus on how to use standard economic evaluation techniques for public health interventions. There are many other text books that cover this.

The Real World

The real world is messy. In many cases, there is not the money, time, or resources to properly evaluate public health policies and interventions to determine if they are cost-effective or if an alternative policy or standard practice should be continued. In this book we try to introduce readers to the techniques that are commonly used in evaluation. We provide examples explaining how 'off the shelf' methodology has been amended to provide a best guess whether a policy or intervention is cost-effective. Practitioners and future practitioners will hopefully gain the toolkit they need to make a difference in the real world.

In Chap. 2, we introduce different types of data that are available to address public health type questions and provide an overview of how to prepare the data for analysis. We focus on datasets, which are readily accessible and publicly available, that will reduce the costs of performing any analysis.

In Chap. 3, a number of methods that can be used to evaluate public health policy *ex post* and *ex ante* using econometric techniques are introduced.

In Chap. 4, we explore how the economist's toolkit for evaluation of interventions can be modified and further developed to be appropriate for public health interventions.

Questions to Consider

1. Find an article in the popular press that identifies a market failure related to either public health or the provision of health care. Has anything been done to alleviate this failure? Can you think of any way to alleviate this failure?
2. Why is it important to distinguish between technical and allocative efficiency before undertaking an economic evaluation? Can you think of a question that could be addressed by allocative or technical efficiency?

3. Why should we not use standard economic evaluation techniques to evaluate public health interventions or policy?

References

Carande-Kulis, V. G., Getzen, T. E., & Thacker, S. B. (2007). Public goods and externalities: A research agenda for public health economics. *Journal of Public Health Management and Practice, 13*(2), 227–232.

Devlin, N. J., Hansen, P., Kind, P., & Williams, A. (2003). Logical inconsistencies in survey respondents' health state valuations—A methodological challenge for estimating social tariffs. *Health Economics, 12*(7), 529–544.

Kaptchuk, T. J. (2001). The double-blind, randomized, placebo-controlled trial: Gold standard or golden calf? *Journal of Clinical Epidemiology, 54*(6), 541–549.

Torrance, G. W., & Feeny, D. (1989). Utilities and quality-adjusted life years. *International Journal of Technology Assessment in Health Care, 5*(4), 559–575.

Wakefield, A. J., Murch, S. H., Anthony, A., Linnell, J., Casson, D. M., Malik, M., … Valentine, A. (1998). RETRACTED: Ileal-lymphoid-nodular hyperplasia, non-specific colitis, and pervasive developmental disorder in children.

Additional Reading

Drummond, M. F., Sculpher, M. J., Claxton, K., Stoddart, G. L., & Torrance, G. W. (2015). *Methods for the economic evaluation of health care programmes.* Oxford University Press. Chapter 4: Principles of Economic Evaluation.

Drummond, M. F., Sculpher, M. J., Claxton, K., Stoddart, G. L., & Torrance, G. W. (2015). *Methods for the economic evaluation of health care programmes.* Oxford University Press. Chapter 3: Critical Assessment of Economic Evaluation.

Guiness, L., & Wiseman, V. (2005). *Introduction to health economics. Understanding public health* (2nd ed.). Maidenhead: Open University Press. Chapter 13: What is Economic Evaluation and What Questions Can It Help to Answer?

Part II

Data

This section consists of two chapters. Chapter 2 discusses the different types of data available for research. Chapter 3 outlines how non-response and a lack of following up may impact on your findings, and how to control for these.

2

Observational Data

Learning Outcomes:

* Discuss one benefit of secondary data
* Identify the main types of observational data available
* Discuss the pros and cons of each type of data
* Define cross-sectional and longitudinal data
* Identify one benefit of data linkage

The Rise of Big Data

Improvements in computer technology mean that it is now possible to store and analyse large datasets. This availability of 'big data' has opened up opportunities for the analysis of public health questions in a way that was not possible even ten years ago. Additionally, using pre-collected data is significantly cheaper than primary data collection.

Secondary data has an important role to play in public health. Observational data can be used to understand your population. For example, is smoking positively and significantly associated with different indicators of socioeconomic status such as educational attainment,

© The Author(s) 2018
H. Brown, *The Economics of Public Health*,
https://doi.org/10.1007/978-3-319-74826-9_2

household income, and/or area-level deprivation? Is physical activity participation associated with availability of green space and sports facilities? Before you make any intervention, you need to make sure that the behaviour/factor that you are targeting is associated with your outcome of interest, and what this association is—is it a positive or negative association? Additionally, secondary data can be used for forecasting, such as using current trends to predict obesity, smoking rates, and physical activity participation in the future. In sum, it can help with the context of your research and provide important background information that will motivate your intervention.

Natural experiments are becomingly increasingly popular in the public health world. Evaluation techniques that we will discuss in Chap. 3 allow you to evaluate a local or regional intervention without having data from before the intervention, as long as you have other data available from regions/areas that were not subject to the intervention. In other cases, a before/after analysis can be done quickly and cheaply using secondary data. With the right dataset you may not even need an intervention to understand how social/environmental factors may have led to a certain outcome. You can use secondary datasets to generate an alternative scenario. This will be discussed in greater detail in Chap. 4.

Many primary data studies are not powered to identify intervention-related inequalities, such as if an intervention targeted at reducing smoking rates was more successful with those from higher socioeconomic groups than lower socioeconomic groups—thereby actually increasing health inequalities. With an appropriate dataset it would be possible to use economic modelling to forecast at population level how it would change smoking rates at a national level if the intervention was rolled out. This would give you the opportunity to perform sub-group analysis by socioeconomic status to understand if there are differential outcomes between groups.

In order to know what questions to answer, the first thing you need to understand is what data is out there. There are a number of different types of datasets available to analyse public health questions.

Administrative data is not primarily collected for research purposes but for administrative purposes. It is usually collected by government or other organisations, such as health providers, for the purpose of registration, transaction, and record keeping, usually during the delivery of a service.

In many countries such as the UK, USA, Canada, Australia, Sweden, Finland, and Denmark government departments are the main purveyors of large administrative datasets, including such things as welfare, tax, health, educational record systems, and census data. Historically, these datasets have been used to produce official statistics and inform policy-making. The potential for this type of data to be used for social science research is being increasingly acknowledged but has so far not been fully exploited. However, health research has embraced administrative data, some examples of public health publications such these datasets are as follows:

Elliott, A. F., Davidson, A., Lum, F., Chiang, M. F., Saaddine, J. B., Zhang, X., … Chou, C. F. (2012). Use of electronic health records and administrative data for public health surveillance of eye health and vision-related conditions in the United States. *American Journal of Ophthalmology, 154*(6), S63–S70.

This study proposes how an eye surveillance system can be developed using electronic health records in the USA.

The second example, also from the USA, is a study that uses the insurance claims by 1.5 million adult members from the Blue Cross Blue Shield of Minnesota plan, in order to estimate the number of insurance claims related to physical inactivity:

Garrett, N. A., Brasure, M., Schmitz, K. H., Schultz, M. M., & Huber, M. R. (2004). Physical inactivity: Direct cost to a health plan. *American Journal of Preventive Medicine, 27*(4), 304–309.

The final example, from Sweden, uses administrative data to estimate the relationship between a sudden change in wealth and health outcomes in an individual's health, as well as the health and development of their children:

Cesarini, D., Lindqvist, E., Östling, R., & Wallace, B. (2016). Wealth, health, and child development: Evidence from administrative data on Swedish lottery players. *The Quarterly Journal of Economics*, qjw001.

There are a number of advantages and disadvantages associated with using administrative data to answer public health questions (Smith et al. 2004).

Advantages of Using Administrative Data

1. Administrative datasets are typically very large, covering a breadth of individuals and time periods that cannot normally be covered by other survey methods because of financial or logistical reasons.
2. Usually no additional or minimum cost associated with using this type of dataset.
3. Scope of administrative data allows a large number of different research questions to be answered.
4. Consistent data collection over time.
5. Data are subject to rigorous quality checks.
6. Possibility of obtaining near 100% cover of the population of interest.
7. Large coverage means that it may be possible to explore the impact of policies at local or regional level.
8. Possibility of capturing individuals who may not respond to survey.
9. Control groups can be specified ad hoc (we will discuss this in greater detail later in this section)
10. Potential for data linkage with other datasets, which could be administrative or another type of survey or data, to produce a powerful research resource.

Disadvantages of Administrative Data

1. Lack of researcher control over content of data. The information collected is limited to that required for administrative purposes, such as that related to service use or administrative definitions.
2. Proxy indicators for a variable of interest sometimes need to be used because the true variable of interest is not collected as part of the administrative data.

3. The data may lack contextual factors such as socioeconomic characteristics, such as type of employment, hours worked, and wages, which may be important for the research question.
4. Changes to administrative procedures may change the definition of variables, making longitudinal analysis problematic.
5. There is the possibility of missing or erroneous data being entered into the database.
6. Quality issues with data that are deemed unimportant for the administrative purpose of the dataset (e.g. address of participant).
7. Possibility of data protection issues regarding the use of data.
8. Access to data for researchers is dependent upon receiving support of the administrators of the data.
9. Possibility of underdeveloped theory and methods in data collection.

If you are interested in finding out about administrative data that can be used for research, the links that follow will be of some use. It is worth noting that some organisations such as the European Union (EU), the Organisation for Economic Cooperation and Development (OECD), and the World Health Organisation (WHO) also collect administrative data related to health that can potentially be used for analysis exploring cross-country differences. This list is by no means complete.

Country	Website
Netherlands	https://www.cbs.nl/en-gb
Canada	http://www.statcan.gc.ca/eng/start
Sweden	http://www.scb.se/en_/
UK	http://www.adls.ac.uk/find-administrative-data/
Australia	http://www.abs.gov.au/browse?opendocument&ref=topBar
USA	http://www.census.gov/topics/health.html
EU	http://ec.europa.eu/eurostat/web/health/health-care/data/
OECD	http://www.oecd.org/els/health-systems/health-data.htm

The next type of dataset that we will discuss is *Household Surveys*. These collect information from one to all members of a household. They can collect data on any population-based subject, examples including health, health behaviour, well-being, economic outcomes and behaviours, environmental attitudes, and voting behaviour. Household surveys provide

not only important socioeconomic and demographic statistics to comple-
ment census data but they also capture how people currently live. They
are therefore an important tool in answering a multitude of research
questions, ranging from explaining the determinants of a specific behaviour and identifying at risk groups in a population to evaluating policy or
forecasting outcomes of potential policy.

Household surveys can be collected on an annual, biannual, or even on
a five-yearly basis. The same household can be asked a number of times
or the survey can be issued to different households on each occasion. If
different households are asked to respond to the survey, this is usually
referred to as *cross-sectional* data. This type of household data can be used
to look at a range of questions. Examples include:

1. The relationship between obesity and employment

   Morris, S. (2007). The impact of obesity on employment. *Labour
   Economics, 14*(3), 413–433.

2. The impact of the smoking bans on exposure to secondhand smoke in
   children

   Jarvis, M. J., Sims, M., Gilmore, A., & Mindell, J. (2011). Impact of
   smoke-free legislation on children's exposure to secondhand smoke:
   Cotinine data from the Health Survey for England. *Tobacco Control*,
   tc-2010.

3. To analyse if having more and better drugs keeps people out of
   hospital

   Lichtenberg, F. R. (1996). Do (more and better) drugs keep people
   out of hospitals? *The American Economic Review, 86*(2), 384–388.

Some examples of cross-sectional datasets that may be of use in addressing economics of public health questions are:

Dataset	Link	Country
Health Survey for England	https://data.gov.uk/dataset/health_survey_for_england	England
Medical Expenditure Panel Survey	https://meps.ahrq.gov/mepsweb/	USA
National Health and Nutrition Examination Survey	https://www.cdc.gov/nchs/nhanes/	USA
Living Costs and Food Survey	https://discover.ukdataservice.ac.uk/series/?sn=2000028	UK

It would be possible to pool together multiple years of cross-sectional data, as in the Lichtenberg (1996) paper cited above, in order to look at trends in health outcomes and drug usage at population level. However, this does not allow you to investigate differences at individual level, since you only have one year of data for each individual. To do this you need *panel* or *longitudinal* data. This is when the same households respond to a survey over time. There are many benefits to this. Because you have repeated observations for the same individuals, you have a large number of data points, increasing the degree of freedom—which means more complex model structures can be estimated. This also allows you to control for some common types of bias, such as endogeneity, which we will discuss in greater detail in Chap. 4. In addition, you can answer important questions about which cross-sectional population-level data may give misleading information, for example, exploring individual retirement decisions in relation to health:

Cai, L. (2010). The relationship between health and labour force participation: Evidence from a panel data simultaneous equation model. *Labour Economics, 17*(1), 77–90.

Jones, A. M., Rice, N., & Roberts, J. (2010). Sick of work or too sick to work? Evidence on self-reported health shocks and early retirement from the BHPS. *Economic Modelling, 27*(4), 866–880.

The relationship between debt and depression:

Bridges, S., & Disney, R. (2010). Debt and depression. *Journal of Health Economics, 29*(3), 388–403.

Gathergood, J. (2012). Debt and depression: Causal links and social norm effects. *The Economic Journal, 122*(563), 1094–1114.

Or early life factors on labour market outcomes in adulthood:

Case, A., Fertig, A., & Paxson, C. (2005). The lasting impact of childhood health and circumstance. *Journal of Health Economics, 24*(2), 365–389.

Black, S. E., Devereux, P. J., & Salvanes, K. G. (2007). From the cradle to the labor market? The effect of birth weight on adult outcomes. *The Quarterly Journal of Economics, 122*(1), 409–439.

Smith, J. P. (2009). The impact of childhood health on adult labor market outcomes. *The Review of Economics and Statistics, 91*(3), 478–489.

Cons of Panel Data

A potential downside of using panel data is *sample attrition*. This is when individuals leave the sample because they have lost interest, moved away, or died. Over time this can change the representativeness of the sample, which may impact on the generalisability of any research findings when using a panel dataset. Many studies include sample weights which can be used to combat for sample attrition. However, these may not be appropriate for all research questions. In Chap. 3, we will discuss a number of methods to test for and control for sample attrition.

Data Linkage

Another important resource for addressing public health questions is linked data. This type of data can combine different datasets to permit the researcher to look at specific health outcomes such as hospital admissions, pregnancy outcomes, educational outcomes, or any other outcome of interest collected by an administrative data service. Linked data can be a powerful tool to allow you to predict outcomes of potential policy or evaluate an existing policy without having to do costly primary data collection. There are several types.

It is possible to link two administrative datasets. This will usually provide a large number of observations, and these may allow you to estimate the causal effect of a policy by comparing regions if the policy has not been implemented nationally at the same time. One example would be looking at quit rates around the smoking ban, comparing Scotland and England: the ban was enforced in Scotland in March 2006 and in England in July 2007. Additionally, it will allow you to identify regional differences in outcomes, which may mean that it is more cost-effective for an intervention to be targeted at a specific area.

The link provided here provides information regarding the data that is available for linkage in the UK: http://www.adls.ac.uk/find-administrative-data/linked-administrative-data/linkage-of-administrative-datasets/.

In the USA, much health usage and insurance data is held by private companies, and this may have an impact on your ability to access some data. Information about using linked administrative data can be found here: www.census.gov/about/adrm/linkage/guidance.html.

Dataset linkage can involve an exact linkage of individuals between datasets to give a rich overview of individual outcomes; or alternatively different individuals can be matched between datasets using propensity score matching (which we will discuss further in Chap. 3). This matches individuals between datasets who share key characteristics of interest such as age, income, and educational attainment. This is based on the assumption that these key characteristics of interest will influence the outcome that you are concerned with, say hospital admission for risky drinking.

Alternatively, household surveys can be linked to administrative datasets. These are powerful tools which include the rich information that is collected in household surveys plus outcomes collected in administrative data. These datasets can be used to investigate a wide range of topics such as inequalities in educational outcomes, risky drinking, hospital admissions, and incidence of disease. They can also be used for policy evaluation or policy prediction to understand how people with specific characteristics of interest, such as socioeconomic status, may react to a policy change, or how a policy might have affected their outcomes. It is worth noting that not everyone in the household survey may have given permission for their data to be linked, which may affect the generalisability of your findings. The link above for the UK gives details of household surveys that can be linked to administrative datasets. American datasets such as the PSID can be linked with some administrative datasets. Many of these linked datasets require special licence agreements with the data provider, and may have a fee associated with their use or special requirements for where the data can be accessed or stored.

Questions to Consider

1. You are tasked with investigating the determinants of a teen pregnancy to identify what factors an intervention to curb teen pregnancy rates should focus on. In an ideal world which type of data would you want to investigate this research question?
2. Explain how sample attrition may bias your results.
3. Discuss two weaknesses of using administrative data.

References and Further Reading

Smith, G., Noble, M., Anttila, C., Gill, L., Zaidi, A., Wright, G., … Barnes, H. (2004). The value of linked administrative records for longitudinal analysis, Report to the ESRC National Longitudinal Strategy Committee Van den. In *Unemployment dynamics and duration dependence in France, the Netherlands and the United Kingdom, in "The Economic Journal".*

3

Missing Data and Sample Attrition

Learning Outcomes:

* Identify if data is missing at random
* Conduct a test to determine if the dataset suffers from sample attrition
* Define multiple imputation
* Define Inverse Probability Weighting (IPW)
* Apply multiple imputation (MI) method
* Apply inverse probability weighting
* Compare and contrast MI and IPW

Missing at Random or Missing at Non-Random

There are two main causes of missing data. Data can be *missing at random* (MAR). For example, an individual forgot to fill in a question or missed a page of a questionnaire. Data can also be *non-random missing data* (NMAR). This is the case if an individual specifically did not answer a question. This may be because they did not want to share the information, thought the question was irrelevant, or had just grown bored with the survey. A large amount of data that is missing at random can lead you

© The Author(s) 2018
H. Brown, *The Economics of Public Health*,
https://doi.org/10.1007/978-3-319-74826-9_3

to the Type 2 error of incorrectly thinking a variable is not significant because the sample size is too small. If data is not missing at random this may lead to results that are not generalisable to the population of interest, leading you to possibly draw incorrect conclusions. There are a number of different ways to deal with missing data depending upon whether it is MAR or NMAR.

Sample Attrition

Unlike with the cross-sectional data where new participants are recruited each year to keep the sample representative of the population of interest, without reboosting a panel sample the data will become less representative of the population of interest over time. This is because of *sample attrition*, where participants leave the sample either because of a lack of interest, moving area, illness, or death. This could affect interpretation of your findings.

Our Example

To gain a better understanding of how missing data or sample attrition may affect your findings, in this chapter we will work through the following example:

* Suppose you want to know if there is a relationship between smoking and socioeconomic status.

You have six years of data from the Household Income and Labour Dynamics of Australia Survey (HILDA). The HILDA is a longitudinal nationally representative dataset of the Australian population which asks all individuals in the household to complete a questionnaire on demographic characteristics, employment, health, and opinions and attitudes. Each individual completes a questionnaire on a yearly basis. If individuals move to a new household they continue to participate in the survey. For more information about how the HILDA is constructed see Wooden and Watson (2007). Because we have six years of data there are two problems that could affect our data: sample attrition and NMAR. If our data suffers from attrition missing and/or NMAR this could lead us to draw incorrect conclusions regarding the relationship between smoking and socioeconomic status.

It is worth noting that there are a number of ways to measure socioeconomic status and there is not a fixed definition of what it constitutes. In our analysis we are going to focus on socioeconomic status measured by area-level deprivation. The reason why this is chosen is because if we can identify whether smokers live in specific areas it will be easier to develop interventions to target these areas. If we were to focus on other indicators of socioeconomic status, such as educational attainment or household income, it would be more difficult to tailor interventions for these individuals because they are not easily identifiable in the real world.

A basic check to determine if your sample may suffer from attrition bias is to develop a simple table that shows the distribution of your sample over the study period of interest, if your key variables are MAR and NMAR for each year of data. To do this the first thing to do is generate a variable which I will call insamp (note that the code below is for STATA and is adapted from Jones et al. 2007):

```
gen insamp=0

replace insamp=1 if wave==1 & smokes==. & most_deprived==1
|wave==2 & smokes==. & most_deprived==1 |wave==3 & smokes==. &
most_deprived==1|wave==4 & smokes==. & most_deprived==1|wave==5 &
smokes==. & most_deprived==1|wave==6 & smokes==. & most_
deprived==1|

gen miss=insamp
replace miss=. if insamp==1

program define table
{
quietly sum miss if wave==1
scalar N0=r(N)
forvalues j=1(1)6{
display "wave=="`j'
quietly sum miss if (wave==`j'-1)
scalar N1=r(N)
```

```
quietly sum miss if (wave==`j' & miss[_n-1]~=.)
scalar N2=r(N)
quietly sum miss if (wave==`j' & miss[_n-1]==.)
scalar N3=r(N)
quietly sum miss if (wave==`j')
scalar N4=r(N)
scalar dropout=N1-N2
scalar rejoiner=N3
scalar rattr=((N1-N2)/N1)
scalar nattr=((N1-N4)/N1)
scalar surv=N4/N0
display "No. individuals at wave= "`j'-1 "="N1
display "No. individuals at wave= "`j' "="N4
display "Survival rate = "surv "Dropouts= "dropout "Rejoiners=
"rejoiner
display "Raw attrition rate="rattr "Net attrition rate= "nattr
display " "
}
}
end
```

Table 3.1 that is generated is the output from the above, and shows if there is sample attrition and if smoking is our key variable of interest in MAR or NMAR, given an individual is of a lower socioeconomic status based upon an area-level deprivation index (most_deprived).

Table 3.1 Sample size, drop outs, rejoiners, survival rate (%) raw and net attrition rate (%)

Wave	No. individuals	Drop outs	Rejoiners	Survival rate (%)	Raw attrition (%)	Net attrition (%)
1	13,350	—	—	—	—	—
2	16,257	1066	3973	121	0.7	−21
3	15,680	1170	593	87.1	7.2	3.5
4	15,273	917	510	84.5	5.8	2.6
5	15,489	388	604	94.4	2.5	−1.4
6	15,595	493	599	92.3	3.1	−0.01

Notes: Drop outs are non-respondents at wave t and respondents and wave $t - 1$. Rejoiners are respondents at wave t and non-respondents at wave $t - 1$. Raw attrition rates exclude rejoiners. Net attrition rates include rejoinders. Table controls for item non-response in the smoking and area-level disadvantage variables

Sample Attrition

From the table we can see that the net attrition rate is relatively low, as there appears to be a significant boosting of the sample during this period. Table 3.1 suggests that attrition should not bias our findings; but we still may be concerned that missing variables could impact on our conclusions. So now we will discuss some regression methods that we can use to determine and correct for missing variables, which lead us to draw incorrect conclusions.

The first step would be to estimate a simple model where you assume that attrition does not bias your results. As smoking is a binary variable, we would want to use a binary response model such as a probit or logit. For large samples probit and logit models should give the same results in terms of the sign and significance of the coefficients. The main difference is that probits assume a cumulative normal distribution function and logits assume a cumulative logistical distribution.

As can be seen in Fig. 3.1, the predicted values for the two models are pretty similar. Looking again at Table 3.1 , we can see that the logit model has fatter tails, which will mean that the coefficients will be larger in logit models when compared with probit models. But there is no statistical reason to prefer one model over the other. Economists tend to prefer probit models and medical researchers tend to prefer logit models, as the interpretation of odds ratios is more intuitive than marginal effects.

In our example we will estimate a logit model using the *logit* command in STATA v.14 and the cluster command, to control for the fact that the same individuals appear in our sample more than once. The STATA output from this regression equation is shown in Table 3.2.

Table 3.2 shows the odds ratios for our model of the relationship between smoking and socioeconomic status. Looking at this, we can say that those who are living in the most deprived areas are more likely to be smokers. Both higher levels of income and higher levels of educational attainment compared with having no qualifications are associated with a lower likelihood of being a smoker. But to make sure that we are not drawing incorrect conclusions for the population as a whole, we should re-estimate the model.

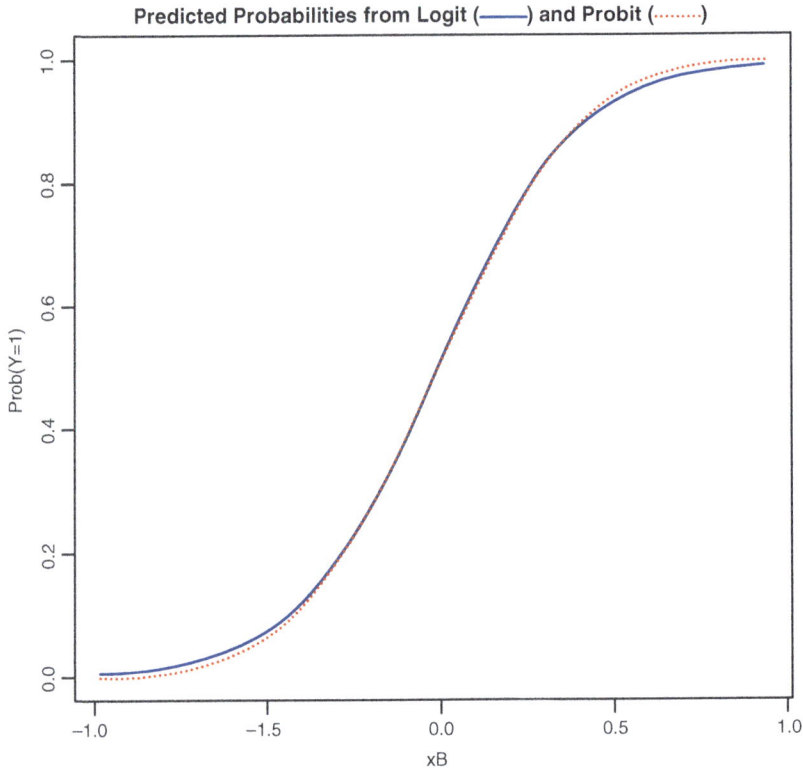

Fig. 3.1 Estimated predicted probabilities from logit and probit models

Multiple Imputation

This method replaces each missing value with a set of plausible values that represent the uncertainty around which value to impute (Rubin 1987; Yuan 2010). Each missing variable can be imputed from the variable mean of complete cases (i.e. individuals who gave a response). The data that has been multiply imputed is then analysed using standard procedures for complete data, and the results from the different imputations are then pooled. Any findings would then no longer suffer from attrition bias as the results reflect the uncertainty from the missing values. For our missing imputation results, we are going to impute values for household

Table 3.2 Odds ratios using complete cases

```
Logistic regression                        Number of obs   =    39,544
                                           Wald chi2(8)    =    496.75
                                           Prob > chi2     =    0.0000
Log pseudolikelihood = -16737.321          Pseudo R2       =    0.0643
```

(Std. Err. adjusted for 8,279 clusters in pid)

smokes_m	Odds Ratio	Robust Std. Err.	z	P>|z|	[95% Conf. Interval]	
highschool_m	.5905974	.0490814	-6.34	0.000	.5018254	.6950729
degree_m_m	.222805	.0217548	-15.38	0.000	.1839981	.2697966
diploma_m	.4417151	.0527715	-6.84	0.000	.349502	.5582579
cert1_4_m	.9355765	.0742244	-0.84	0.401	.8008456	1.092974
disadvantaged_m	1.573562	.090468	7.89	0.000	1.405873	1.761252
loghhincome_m	.7561382	.0292653	-7.22	0.000	.7009008	.8157288
employed_m	1.182344	.0615102	3.22	0.001	1.067729	1.309262
unemployed_m	1.675008	.1660762	5.20	0.000	1.379179	2.034292
_cons	3.622544	1.357332	3.44	0.001	1.738108	7.550063

income. Compared with other indicators of socioeconomic status included in our model (educational attainment and index of area-level multiple deprivation), household income has the highest percentage of missing values. Multiple imputations can be undertaken using most common statistical software packages. Here is a simple guide to get you started using MI in Stata v.14.

- First, what you need to do is load your data into STATA.
- Next, let STATA know that you want to impute missing data (to do this type *mi set long*—it can be flong or mlong or even wide depending on your dataset).
- Tell STATA what variables you want to be imputed (household income in our case) *mi register imputed loghhincome_m*.
- It is good practice to then set a seed so that the results are reproducible (*set seed 90051102*). The seed can be any set of random numbers; it is just so that anyone can replicate your results exactly by using the same seed. In theory if the seed is not set then the results could be slightly different each time, as the statistical software package would potentially draw different data to estimate the model.

Table 3.3 Multiple imputations

```
Performing EM optimization:
note: 131 observations omitted from EM estimation because of all imputation variables missing
  observed log likelihood =   1652.697 at iteration 1

Performing MCMC data augmentation ...

Multivariate imputation              Imputations =      10
Multivariate normal regression            added =      10
Imputed: m=1 through m=10               updated =       0

Prior: uniform                       Iterations =    1000
                                        burn-in =     100
                                        between =     100
```

	Observations per *m*			
Variable	Complete	Incomplete	Imputed	Total
loghhincome_m	41262	173	131	41435

```
(complete + incomplete = total; imputed is the minimum across m
of the number of filled-in observations.)

Note: Right-hand-side variables (or weights) have missing values;
      model parameters estimated using listwise deletion.
```

- Next we create a *N* number of imputations. In our case we will create ten (Table 3.3).
- *mi impute mvn loghhincome_m = smokes_m highschool_m degree_m_m diploma_m cert1_4_m employed_m unemployed_m married_m disadvantaged_m , add(10)*
- Finally, the model is estimated separately on each of the ten imputations, and then these results are combined by estimating a logistic regression.
- *mi estimate: logistic smokes_m highschool_m degree_m_m diploma_m cert1_4_m disadvantaged_m loghhincome_m employed_m unemployed_m married_m*

Note that the coefficients are shown if we want to display the odds ratio you would need to type the command

mi estimate, or

Table 3.4 Logistic regression output using multiple imputations

```
Multiple-imputation estimates              Imputations       =        10
Logistic regression                        Number of obs     =    31,206
                                           Average RVI       =    0.0005
                                           Largest FMI       =    0.0048
DF adjustment:    Large sample             DF:      min      = 387,375.78
                                                    avg      =  1.27e+13
                                                    max      =  1.27e+14
Model F test:     Equal FMI                F(   9, 2.4e+08)  =    199.24
Within VCE type:        OIM                Prob > F          =    0.0000
```

smokes_m	Odds Ratio	Std. Err.	t	P>|t|	[95% Conf. Interval]	
highschool_m	.5374898	.0245828	-13.57	0.000	.4914048	.5878968
degree_m_m	.1872055	.0108386	-28.94	0.000	.1671233	.2097009
diploma_m	.4339401	.0268942	-13.47	0.000	.3843042	.4899869
cert1_4_m	.9179	.0392988	-2.00	0.045	.844019	.9982482
disadvantaged_m	1.67956	.0573866	15.18	0.000	1.570768	1.795888
loghhincome_m	.7071902	.0199113	-12.31	0.000	.6692219	.7473127
employed_m	1.160647	.0416104	4.16	0.000	1.081892	1.245136
unemployed_m	1.671485	.1616533	5.31	0.000	1.382868	2.020338
married_m	.3019926	.0810274	-4.46	0.000	.1784888	.5109538
_cons	23.75796	8.996838	8.37	0.000	11.31018	49.90552

Comparing Table 3.4 where we use MI and Table 3.2 where we use complete cases, we can see that the magnitude of the odds ratios are relatively similar and suggest the same thing. Higher income and a greater level of educational attainment are associated with a lower likelihood of being a smoker, whereas living in a deprived area is associated with a higher likelihood of being a smoker.

Another method to deal with data that is not missing at random is *Inverse Probability Weighting* (IPW). This method can also correct for unequal sampling fractions of the population in your data if it is not representative of the population as a whole. This could be especially important when answering public health research questions. When using IPW, the analysis model is only fitted to complete cases (as you would do if you did not think sample attrition or missing variables were an issue), but more weight is given to some respondents with complete cases than others—specifically individuals with the key characteristics of interest, in our case those from lower socioeconomic groups. For IPW this will be measured by area-level deprivation.

Using statistical software packages such as STATA v.14, IPW can be estimated as a two-stage model. It is worth noting that both stages are estimated simultaneously. This means that we do not need to correct the standard errors to reflect uncertainty around the predicted treatment probabilities. The first stage is to estimate our relationship of interest between smoking status and socioeconomic position measured by log of household income whilst also controlling for educational attainment, marital status, employment status, and area-level deprivation.

A logit model is used to estimate the parameters of the treatment model and calculate the inverse probability weights. The second stage uses the estimated inverse probability weights to compute weighted averages of the likelihood of being a smoker (outcome) for each observation of household income (treatment). All potential observed outcomes (contrasts) of these weighted averages provide the estimates for the average treatment effects (ATEs).

IPW can be estimated in STATA v.14 using the command *teffects*. An example for the relationship between smoking and socioeconomic status is shown in Table 3.5.

What this shows is that those in the most disadvantaged areas measured by an index of area-level deprivation are significantly more likely to smoke. The likelihood of someone being a smoker if they live in the most deprived area is 27%, which is 9% higher than if they lived in a less deprived area.

Table 3.5 Inverse probability weights–average treatment effects

```
. *IPW
. teffects ipw (disadvantaged_m) (smokes_m  university_m post_hs_m highschool_m loghhincome_m employed_m unemployed_m marrie
> d_m, logit),atet

Iteration 0:   EE criterion =  7.899e-20
Iteration 1:   EE criterion =  7.436e-33

Treatment-effects estimation                   Number of obs     =      8,402
Estimator      : inverse-probability weights
Outcome model  : weighted mean
Treatment model: logit
```

disadvantag~m	Coef.	Robust Std. Err.	z	P>|z|	[95% Conf. Interval]	
ATET						
smokes_m						
(1 vs 0)	.0912681	.0136366	6.69	0.000	.0645408	.1179954
POmean						
smokes_m						
0	.2703738	.0069455	38.93	0.000	.2567608	.2839868

This highlights that the different methods for dealing with different datasets give you slightly different answers to the question about the relationship between smoking and socioeconomic status. The complete case and MI methods tell you what the relationship is between multiple indicators of socioeconomic status such as educational attainment, household income, area-level deprivation, and smoking status. The conclusion that we can draw from this is that all our indicators of socioeconomic status being on the lower end of these measures increases the likelihood of being a smoker.

The IPW method focuses specifically on whether smoking is positively/negatively related with area-level deprivation. Results indicate that those in the most deprived areas are significantly more likely to smoke than those in less deprived areas.

In sum we can say that those from lower socioeconomic groups are more likely to smoke. Individuals living in the most deprived areas are more likely to be smokers. There may be an opportunity to reduce health inequalities by targeting interventions to reduce smoking rates at those living in the most deprived areas. Interpreting your results correctly is important for drawing any sort of policy recommendation/conclusions from your analysis.

Pros and Cons of MI vs IPW for Public Health Research

The MI method specifies an imputation model based upon the distribution of missing data given the observed data. Missing values are replaced by random generation to create complete cases. This is done repeatedly to create several imputed datasets. The model is fitted to each of these imputed datasets and the estimated parameters are averaged over the dataset. This differs from IPW, which estimates a model for the probability that an individual is a complete case (Seaman and White 2013). The equation is then estimated on complete cases, which are weighted for the probability that an individual is not in the sample.

MI has Two Advantages over IPW

An IPW model of missingness will only use data on fully observed variables unless

1. The pattern of missing data is monotone-if Xi is missing then all variables Xj are missing where j>i.
2. Or if a more complicated Markov RMM is utilised.

Advantages of IPW

1. IPW requires less technical sophistication than MI.
2. IPW is easier to understand and explain (a big bonus for public health research).
3. Danger of applying MI incorrectly if you are estimating a model with random effects, interaction terms, or quadratics. Commonly used MI methods such as the multivariate normal approach do not allow inclusion of interactions and non-linear terms without defying distributional assumptions, and the chain methods require the user to specify them (Seaman and White 2013).

The key thing to take away from this section is that missingness either through sample attrition or non-response may bias your findings. It is important to be aware of the shortcomings of your data when interpreting the results and making any policy conclusions. Even if you use a method to impute missing data or weight missing data, there are also limitations associated with this that should be acknowledged.

Questions to Consider

1. If data is *missing at random* why will this not bias your results?
2. Give one reason why you would want to employ a multiple imputation method.
3. Outline how you would employ IPW.

References and Further Reading

Jones, A. M., Rice, N., & Bago d'Uva, T. (2007). *Applied health economics*. London: Routledge Advanced Texts in Economics and Finance.

Rubin, D. B. (1987). *Multiple imputation for nonresponse in surveys*. New York: Wiley.

Seaman, S. R., & White, I. R. (2013). Review of inverse probability weighting for dealing with missing data. *Statistical Methods in Medical Research, 22*(3), 278–295.

Wooden, M., & Watson, N. (2007). The HILDA survey and its contribution to economic and social research (so far). *The Economic Record, 83*(261), 208–231.

Yuan, Y. C. (2010). Multiple imputation for missing data: Concepts and new development (Version 9.0). *SAS Institute Inc, Rockville, MD, 49*, 1–11.

Part III

Policy Evaluation

4

Correlations versus Causation

Learning Outcomes:

* Define correlation
* Define causation
* Compare and contrast correlation versus causation

Correlations

Correlations are when there is a statistically significant association between x and y, but you are not certain that x causes y. The statistic from this relationship is called the *correlation coefficient*. A correlation coefficient can be estimated when you have information on at least two variables for the same individual or group. The correlation coefficient describes the direction (i.e. positive or negative) and strength of the relationship. The higher the correlation coefficient the stronger the relationship. A p-value is obtained to determine if the correlation coefficient is statistically significant. To be meaningful this is usually at $p < 0.05$ (95%) or $p < 0.01$ (99%). If the correlation coefficient is not statistically significant then

© The Author(s) 2018
H. Brown, *The Economics of Public Health*,
https://doi.org/10.1007/978-3-319-74826-9_4

this means we cannot be sure that there is no relationship between our variables of interest.

Understanding Correlation Coefficients

A positive correlation coefficient means that if one variable increases the other variable of interest is also likely to increase. A negative correlation coefficient implies that if one variable increases then the other variable is likely to decrease. The stronger the relationship, the more obvious the impact of one variable on the other variable.

Strength of the Correlation

Two factors may be correlated but the magnitude of this correlation is also important. Two variables may be statistically related, but if the magnitude of this correlation is very small then it may not be economically meaningful. For example, if the relationship between meeting the recommended level of physical activity and being educated to degree level or higher is 0.75, $p < 0.001$, we can say that there is a fairly strong association between physical activity and educational attainment. In this scenario it may be worth exploring if it would be worthwhile to develop an intervention to improve educational attainment as a means of improving physical activity participation.

However, if the relationship between the unemployment and smoking was 0.0004 $p < 0.001$; we can only really say that they are significantly correlated; but developing an intervention to reduce unemployment is not likely to have a large reduction on smoking rates or vice versa.

Example

Say you were approached by someone from the Department of Work and Pensions who was interested in understanding the relationship between body fatness and wages to decide if obesity should be a protected charac-

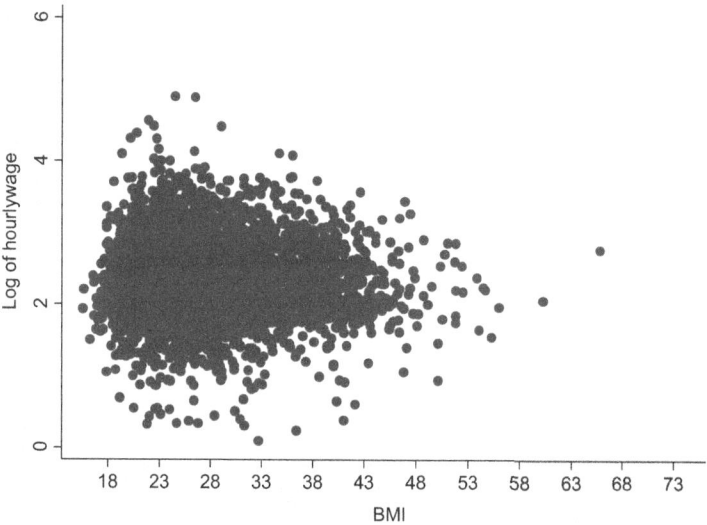

Fig. 4.1 Scatter plot of the relationship between BMI and log of hourly wage for women. The data come from waves 2 and 3 of the Understanding Society Survey, UK (University of Essex 2016)

teristic, in order to reduce any stigma or penalisation in the labour market for people with elevated body fatness. If you were unsure what the relationship was between wages and body fatness measured using body mass index (BMI), before you estimated any models it would be helpful to start with a simple scatter plot to get an idea of what any relationship between BMI and wages might look like (Fig. 4.1).

Using objectively taken data on BMI and self-reported earnings for women from the Understanding Society Survey, UK, we can see that the scatter plot suggests that there may be a negative relationship between BMI and hourly wage. From the graph it does not appear that the relationship is very strong, but you cannot say for certain without estimating a regression equation to give you the magnitude of the correlation coefficient. As a rule of thumb, a stronger relationship is more likely to have a more obvious positive or negative slope between your variables of interest.

Estimating Correlation Coefficients

Carrying on with our example, in which we are looking at the relationship between BMI and self-reported earnings for women, to determine if there was a significant association between BMI and self-reported earnings and the direction of this association, the first step is to estimate a simple regression equation. Formally this can be shown by Eq. 4.1:

$$W_i = \beta_1 X_i + \beta_2 BMI_i + \varepsilon_{it} \qquad (4.1)$$

The wage rate, which we will measure as the log of hourly wage, is determined by a matrix of individual characteristics such as educational attainment, marital status captured by X for individual i, a vector containing BMI, and an error term (which contains all unobserved factors influencing the wage rate).

Results from the model estimated using pooled ordinary least squares (OLS) can be seen in Table 4.1.

The negative relationship that we found in Fig. 4.1 between the hourly wage rate and BMI is found to persistent in a multivariate regression which controls for other factors that are likely to influence the wage rate, and may have possibly reduced the raw correlation that we saw in the graph.

So what can this tell you? Having a higher BMI is associated with a lower wage; but we do not know why. Figure 4.1, which is called a directed acyclic graph (DAG), illustrates the relationship between BMI and the wage rate for women in the UK. It is possible that educational attainment, motivation, or physical appearance may impact on the wage rate. There is some evidence to suggest that individuals who are obese as teenagers have a lower educational attainment, which impacts on their occupation in adulthood and subsequently their wages (Han et al. 2011). However, if you do not have information on weight in adolescence you will not be able to control for this. Other factors such as motivation and physical appearance cannot be easily captured in household surveys (Fig. 4.2).

Table 4.1 Relationship between log of hourly wage and BMI

	Women
	(4)
Log of hourly wage	BMI
Age	0.040*** (0.004)
Age squared	−0.000*** (0.000)
Higher education	0.318*** (0.020)
Some higher education	0.144*** (0.020)
Basic qualifications	0.108*** (0.019)
Ethnic minority	0.018 (0.025)
Urban	0.009 (0.014)
Private sector	−0.105*** (0.013)
Firm size	0.072*** (0.007)
Professionals	0.137*** (0.039)
Intermediate workers	−0.140*** (0.023)
Small employers/own accounts	−0.593*** (0.029)
Lower supervisor/technical	−0.407*** (0.023)
Semi-routine	−0.514*** (0.027)
Routine	−0.640*** (0.037)
BMI	−0.004*** (0.001)
Constant	1.596*** (0.084)
Observations	5159
R-squared	0.403

Robust standard errors in parentheses
*** $p < 0.01$, ** $p < 0.05$, * $p < 0.1$

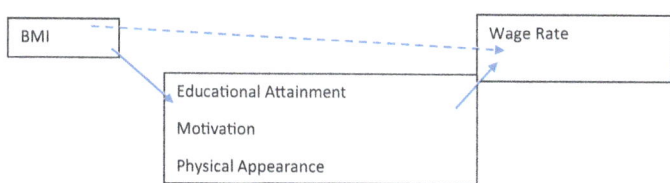

Fig. 4.2   Representation of the relationship BMI and wages for women

What then can you tell the Department of Work and Pensions about including a high BMI as a protected characteristic? The best thing to say would be that there is a negative association between wages and BMI, but you cannot say that a higher BMI necessarily causes lower wages.

Correlation Analysis in Economic Evaluation of Public Health Policy

Why then do we need to do correlation analysis?

There has been a trend in economics to focus solely on estimating causal relationships, as there are clear policy implications from showing that x causes y. However, before you can say that x causes y it is important to show that x and y are associated. Correlation analysis can be very important for setting the scene; for understanding the population of interest, for example. If you were interested in the social and economic determinants of young people's mental health and had a long list of variables to consider, this would be a perfect opportunity to use correlation analysis to determine what factors were important before you tried to establish which specific social determinants were causally related to mental health for intervention development and policy recommendations. Additionally, for new public health problems such as a new synthetic drug that teenagers can purchase on the internet, it is important to first establish if consumption of this drug is associated with negative health outcomes before there is any further analysis or policy recommendations.

Weaknesses of Correlation Analysis

Correlation analysis can lead you to draw false conclusions about possible causal relationships. There is a large literature showing that educational attainment and health are correlated, and it is tempting to say that greater educational attainment leads to better health. There is a simple policy conclusion to draw from this statement: increase the mandatory school leaving age and the population will become healthier. However, to date no research has been able to identify a causal relationship between education and health. The observed association seems to be related to third factors which are independent of education. Therefore, increasing time in education in itself does not seem to lead to improved health outcomes.

Fig. 4.3 Relationship between free swimming and obesity rates

Causal Relationships

Causal relationships are when you can identify if *x* leads to *y*. For example, a programme of free swimming for children aged between four and fifteen in the community reduces obesity in this age group by 15%. Such statements as this can be made if you can make a clear link between the programme (e.g. free swimming) and the outcome of interest (e.g. obesity). This is illustrated in Fig. 4.3.

Causal relationships are useful because they provide clear evidence about what factors policy should focus on or the areas that should be targeted by interventions.

How to Estimate a Causal Relationship

If you have a background in public health, you will probably think that the most robust way to estimate causal relationships is by implementing a Randomised Control Trial (RCT). For example, say you want to establish if, as in Fig. 4.3, free swimming reduces obesity in children between the ages of four and fifteen. What you need to do is first determine what sample size you require that you have the statistical power necessary to be certain of your effect size. The next step is to recruit the required number of children from the population. At the start of the study you will need to collect baseline data on children's socioeconomic status, current weight, swimming habits, and other physical activity participation. Using this baseline data to ensure that the treatment and control groups contained relatively similar children, you then need to randomised children into a free swimming group (treatment) and a paid swimming group (control). Then you need to follow up children for a given length of time, usually about one year, collecting data on how often both the control and treatment group went swimming and how long they swam for. Additionally, data is required on other physical activity and weight over this period. Usually you should collect this information at a few time points (say three, six, nine, and twelve months). At the end of this trial, the data you have collected can be statistically analysed to determine if free swimming for children of this age range significantly reduced obesity rates after controlling for baseline demographic characteristics, weight, and other physical activity throughout the trial period.

As you can probably guess from reading the above paragraph, an RCT is very expensive to undertake—not to mention the time and effort required to collect the data. It is therefore not always possible or feasible to try and estimate causal relationships by using RCTs. They may also be susceptible to systematic errors, leading to biased estimates when generalising to 'real-world' settings, and this is particularly problematic for many public health interventions (Kontopantelis et al. 2015). Additionally, usually because of political reasons, there is often a need to evaluate interventions that have been implemented retrospectively either without randomisation or without a control group (Bernal et al. 2017).

Basic Econometric Tools for Estimating a Causal Relationship

If you are fairly certain that you have data that can control for all the potential confounding factors that may explain the causal relationship between your outcome variable and key variable of interest, then a simple OLS model will give you a causal relationship. For example, suppose you wanted to investigate if there is a causal relationship between being within 1 mile of green space and physical activity participation. You have data on distance from all homes in the local area to green space and demographic and socioeconomic characteristics of all individuals in the local community (Fig. 4.4).

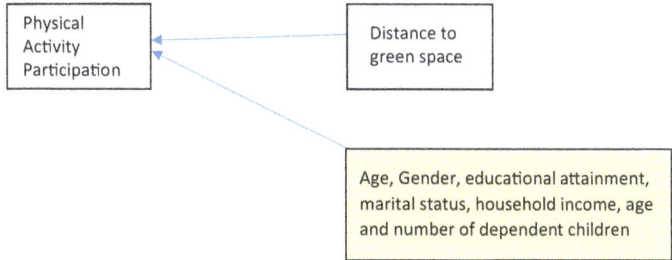

Fig. 4.4 DAG showing relationship between physical activity and distance to green space

If you are certain that all the variables in the yellow box above mediate the relationship between physical activity participation and distance to green space, then you are able to estimate the following model:

$$PA_i = \alpha + \beta_1 \text{Distance}_i + \beta_2 SD_i + \varepsilon,$$

PA_i is physical activity participation for individual i, α is the intercept, β_1 is the coefficient to be estimated on distance to green space, β_2 is the parameter of coefficients on socioeconomic and demographic characteristics, and ε is the error term.

The coefficient on β_1 would be the causal impact of distance from green space on physical activity participation. In practice, we can never be sure that we control for all the potential mediating factors that may influence the relationship we are examining. In the example here it is likely that factors such as motivation may impact on the relationship between distance to green space and physical activity. If this is the case, we are left with correlations from an OLS model, as discussed above.

As highlighted in the example here, with most public health interventions it is not likely that we will be able to find data to control for all potential confounding factors. The most likely types of bias that we will face are:

1. *Omitted Variable Bias*: This is where unobserved factors are correlated with your explanatory variables; for example, thinking about the relationship between education and health. If health was your outcome

variable and education was your independent variable, and you were able to control for age, gender, and socioeconomic status measured as household income, and occupation in your equation, it is likely that unobserved factors such as motivation and ability may be correlated with your education variable, thereby biasing the coefficient.

2. *Measurement Error.* This occurs when variables are measured with error. It may bias the results if measurement error stems from misreporting by respondents; for example, individuals over-reporting their physical activity participation. If there are systematic differences in how individuals misreport key variables by socioeconomic status or the variable of interest, such as those with a higher weight being more likely to misreport their physical activity, this will bias the coefficients.

3. *Reverse Causality/Simultaneity Bias:* This occurs when you are not sure if x causes y or y causes x; for example, if physical activity is influenced by distance to green space or distance to green space influences physical activity participation. Perhaps people who like to exercise choose a home close to green space.

What next? There is not an easy way to capture motivation, and this data is not routinely collected in most of the observational studies available for analysis. One simple thing to do would be to use a fixed effects model specification. This controls for omitted variable bias by removing any bias from the explanatory variables being correlated with time constant unobserved factors which are captured in the error term. This requires you to have multiple years or periods of data; it cannot be done with a cross-section of data:

$$PA_i = \alpha + \bar{\beta}_1 \text{Distance}_i + \bar{\beta}_2 SD_i + \varepsilon$$

What a fixed effect model does is take the means of all variables. If any of these variables are correlated with unobserved factors such as motivation it will remove the bias from this in your model, and again your coefficient on β_1 would be the causal impact of distance to green space on physical activity participation. A weakness of a fixed effects model is that if a variable does not vary over time, such as gender, then the mean will be zero and this variable will be removed from the model. With a fixed effect model, you need to be certain that any potential bias from unobserved factors is constant over time. It is difficult to be 100% sure of this when you are not certain of all the potentially unobserved factors that may influence the relationship between distance to green space and physical activity. A fixed effects framework cannot control for measurement error or simultaneity bias/reverse causality.

Another potential solution would be to use an instrumental variable (IV) model. This is typically used to address the bias from omitted variable bias measurement error and/or reverse causality. An IV approach can be used with cross-sectional or longitudinal data. Carrying on with our example of estimating the causal effect of green space on physical activity participation, what we need to do is identify an instrument that is correlated with distance to green space but none of the other explanatory variables. Say that you chose as an instrument the creation of a new park on a former brownfield site in a local area. Formally this is shown as:

Let Z represent the instrument (new park).

$$(1) \quad \text{cov}\left(\text{Distance}, Z\right) \neq 0$$
$$(2) \quad \text{cov}\left(Z, SD\right) = 0$$

Condition (1) is testable using a basic regression equation (which is usually called the first stage regression), whereas condition (2) is not testable and you need to satisfy your readers/audience that this condition is satisfied. In addition, the instrument should affect all people in the same way. To clarify, the causal chain is:

$$Z_i \quad \rightarrow \quad D_i \quad \rightarrow \quad PA_i,$$

where D_{1i} is equal to an individual's treatment when $Z_i = 1$; and D_{0i} is equal to an individual's treatment when $Z_i = 0$.

If there are defiers (i.e. people who are not affected by the instrument as they should be), effects on compliers could potentially be cancelled out from those on defiers. In your estimation model you could then observe a coefficient of 0 even though the treatment effects may be positive for all those who comply with the intervention. For our instrument this should not be an issue.

Formally the IV approach can be shown as:

First Stage Regression

$$Distance_i = \alpha + \gamma Z + \zeta_i$$

Second Stage Regression:

$$PA_i = \alpha + \beta_1 \hat{D}istance_i + \beta_2 SD + \varepsilon$$

As you can see, in practice IV is typically estimated as *two stage least squares* (2SLS). In most statistical software packages these equations will be estimated simultaneously and the standard errors corrected for any bias from the two stage framework. If the instrument is appropriately specified, then a significant coefficient on β_1 would be from quasi-experimental variation and would thus be exogenous, showing the causal effect of distance to green space on physical activity participation.

In reality it is difficult to find a potential instrument that meets both conditions 1 and 2.

How Do You Know If You Have Found a Good Instrument?

Stock and Yogo (2002) proposed a rule of thumb that an F-statistic over ten, in the first stage equation suggested that your instrument was not weak. However, if you have more than one endogenous variable for which you want to instrument, reporting the first stage F statistics is not enough because one instrument could affect both endogenous variables and the other instrument may not be correlated with the endogenous regressor. In this case your model would be under-identified. In this case you would want to present the Cragg-Donald EV statistic (Cragg and Donald 1993). If you have many IVs to choose from, pick your 'best instrument', that is, the one with the highest F-statistic, and report the just identified model. With many potential instruments for one variable, the weak instrument problem is less problematic.

The other standard test to perform in order to determine if you have appropriate instruments is the Sargen–Hansen test (Hansen 1982; Sargan 1958). This test shows if the instruments should be included as additional regressors in the equation. In other words, it tests the assumption that the instrument is orthogonal to the error term and only indirectly influences the dependent variable.

The simplest test that you can perform is to compare your results from an IV equation to those from an OLS model. If there is not a causal relationship between your potential endogenous regressor of interest and the dependent variable, then there should not be any relationship in the IV model.

If you have chosen weak or inappropriate instruments, then the estimation results will be biased.

Interpreting IV Estimates

As an instrument variable adds a quasi-experimental design to the regression equation, we need to think about how the results from this framework can be interpreted. IV estimates are usually interpreted as the *local average treatment effect* (LATE). LATE is the average effect of distance to green space on physical activity participation for those whose distance to green space has changed as a result of the creation of a new park. The results from an IV equation are therefore not generalisable to the entire population.

The LATE framework divides the population into four groups:

1. Compliers: the sub-section of the population where $D_{1i} = 1$ and $D_{0i} = 0$. Their treatment status (in our case physical activity participation) is affected by the instrument in the hypothesised fashion.
2. Always takers: the sub-population where $D_{1i} = D_{0i} = 1$. They will participate in physical activity irrespective of how far they may have to travel to access a green space.

3. Never takers: the sub-population where $D_{1i} = D_{0i} = 0$. These individuals will not participate in physical activity no matter how close a green space is to their home.
4. The sub-population where $D_{1i} = 0$ and $D_{0i} = 1$. These individuals will only participate in physical activity if they do not have access to green space.

These terms come from the medical literature, where you can think of the treatment as being prescribed a drug. If you use a different instrument the LATE will not be the same.

We could also potentially estimate the average treatment effect on the treated (ATT). This measures the difference in mean outcomes (physical activity participation) between those who were subject to the treatment (creation of a new park) and those who were not subject to the treatment (i.e. the control group). Formally this can be shown as:

$$E\left[PA_{1i} - PA_{0i} | D_i = 1\right] = E\left[PA_{1i} | D_i = 1\right] - E\left[PA_{0i} | D_i = 1\right]$$

The equation above highlights the counterfactual nature of this type of design. The second term is the average physical activity participation for those individuals if they had not been exposed to the creation of a new park, which we cannot observe. Therefore, we use the control group to provide a consistent estimate for this, since we cannot observe the behaviour of someone after they have already been exposed to the intervention.

It is worth noting that because of the two stage framework of the IV approach the standard errors will always be larger. If you do not have appropriate instruments, this may lead to type 2 error, where you erroneously decide that there is not a causal relationship between physical activity participation and green space. If you choose an inappropriate instrument the IV estimates may be more biased than a simple OLS and be less informative about your relationship of interest.

In the next chapter, we will look at how observational data can be organised in a quasi-experimental setup to exploit natural experiments, either where there is some variation in policy or there is data available before and after the implementation of policy to estimate causal effects.

Questions to Consider

1. Why do correlations not show a causal relationship?
2. Give one reason why estimating correlations are useful.
3. Define causation and why it is essential for developing policy.
4. Identify three sources of potential bias in observational data.
5. Identify two methods for interpreting results from an IV model.
6. When would you use a fixed effects model?

References and Further Reading

Bernal, J. L., Cummins, S., & Gasparrini, A. (2017). Interrupted time series regression for the evaluation of public health interventions: A tutorial. *International Journal of Epidemiology, 46*(1), 348–355.

Cragg, J. G., & Donald, S. G. (1993). Testing identifiability and specification in instrumental variable models. *Econometric Theory, 9*(2), 222–240.

Han, E., Norton, E. C., & Powell, L. M. (2011). Direct and indirect effects of body weight on adult wages. *Economics & Human Biology, 9*(4), 381–392.

Hansen, L. P. (1982). Large sample properties of generalized method of moments estimators. *Econometrica, 50*(4): 1029–1054. JSTOR 1912775. https://doi.org/10.2307/1912775

Kontopantelis, E., Doran, T., Springate, D. A., Buchan, I., & Reeves, D. (2015). Regression based quasi-experimental approach when randomisation is not an option: Interrupted time series analysis. *BMJ, 350*, h2750.

Sargan, J. D. (1958). The estimation of economic relationships using instrumental variables. *Econometrica, 26*(3): 393–415. JSTOR 1907619. https://doi.org/10.2307/1907619

Stock, J. H., & Yogo, M. (2002). Testing for weak instruments in linear IV regression.

University of Essex. Institute for Social and Economic Research, NatCen Social Research, Kantar Public. (2016). *Understanding society: Waves 1-6, 2009–2015* [data collection], 8th ed. UK Data Service. SN: 6614, https://doi.org/10.5255/UKDA-SN-6614-9

5

Before and After Study Designs

Learning Outcomes:

* Describe a before and after study design
* Identify three common evaluation methods for before/after study designs in public health
* Interpret the results from these analyses in relation to public health policy

Politics means that many public health interventions/policies are evaluated retrospectively often without a clearly defined control and treatment group. This makes it difficult to establish causality of the intervention on the outcome of interest (Kontopantelis et al. 2015).

In this chapter we will discuss three methods commonly used in public health to evaluate if an intervention has been effective using longitudinal data: (1) Interrupted Time Series (ITS); (2) Regression Discontinuity Approach (RD); and (3) Difference in Difference (DiD). As was mentioned in the previous chapter, it is not always possible to randomise individuals to an intervention and control group or

© The Author(s) 2018
H. Brown, *The Economics of Public Health*,
https://doi.org/10.1007/978-3-319-74826-9_5

undertake an RCT. The approaches that we will discuss in this chapter employ quasi-experimental methods and are 'next best approaches' that can provide useful evidence on the potential effectiveness of an intervention.

Interrupted Time Series

ITS can be used to retrospectively analyse a public health intervention. It is best suited to evaluate interventions targeted at the population level and population level health outcomes over a specific time period. Examples would be a change in the doctor reimbursement system where doctors receive a payment bonus for targeting specific conditions such as diabetes care, hypertension, or smoking cessation (see Kontopantelis et al. 2015) or the introduction of new policy such as a sugar tax which comes into force on a specific date. In this section, we will focus on the second example.

When to Use ITS

There needs to be a clear distinction between the pre- and post-intervention period. For some interventions it may be difficult to define exactly when the intervention began and to distinguish its different components. This does not necessarily mean that the data needs to be able to identify the specific date when the intervention was implemented, but the intervention period needs to be able to be defined in the data to separate out any potential effects of the policy.

The outcomes of interest can either be binary variables, continuous, or count data. ITS works best with short-term outcomes that are likely to change relatively quickly after the introduction of a policy change (Bernal et al. 2017); for example, the amount of dental caries in children after the introduction of a sugar tax. This would be a continuous outcome variable. Other outcomes from the introduction of a sugar tax such as changes in obesity rates may not be appropriate for ITS in the short term, as these are more likely to change gradually.

Data Required to Estimate an ITS

A time series is a continuous sequence of observations on a population taken repeatedly and usually at equal intervals. The data need to cover a sufficient length of time before a change in policy and data points after the change in policy. This span is needed to be able to establish a trend in outcomes which is then 'interrupted' by the change in policy. We have then created a natural experiment where we can compare the trend exhibited in the data before the intervention to the trend in data after the intervention. This is illustrated using hypothetical data on dental caries in children before and after the introduction of a sugar tax in Fig. 5.1. The red line in the graph shows the pre-intervention trend in dental caries in children aged between seven and ten. The dashed part of the line shows the hypothetical or counterfactual scenario of the amount of caries if a sugar tax was not introduced. Given that there are more data points below the counterfactual line after the introduction of the sugar tax this would suggest a reduction in the number of dental caries in children aged seven to ten the first three years after the introduction of a sugar tax.

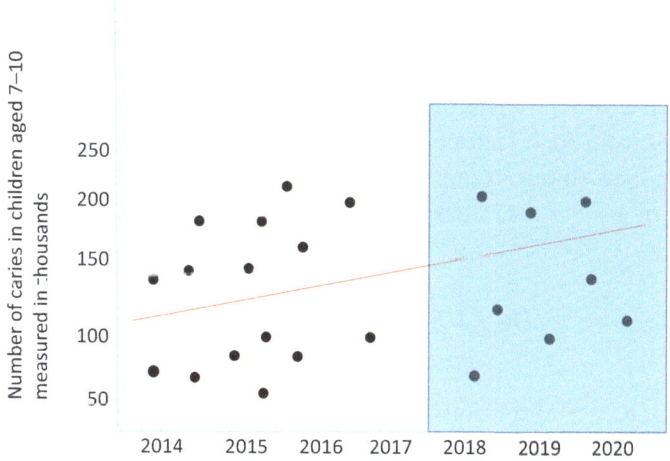

Fig. 5.1 Example of time series data on dental caries in children

Estimating ITS

The basic ITS model is estimated using a regression-based model such as linear, logistic or Poisson. For the example above, we would use a linear model as number of dental caries is a continuous variable. The basic model would include three variables: (1) the pre-intervention slope; (2) the change in level at the intervention point; and (3) the change in slope between pre- and post-intervention.

Next, to improve the reliability of the model you can include variables for sociodemographic characteristics that may impact on childhood caries. It is important to note that the ITS framework will not be biased by time constant variables such as gender. However, with this type of model you cannot control for time varying variables that may be related to the intervention, such as the introduction of fluoride tablets for children around the same time as the introduction of the sugar tax. What this means is that you would not be able to separate out the impact of the sugar tax compared with fluoride tablets using an ITS approach. One way to get around this problem would be to add a control group to the analysis which has not been affected by the additional intervention.

ITS framework is also subject to biases associated with estimating linear and logistic regressions such as serial autocorrelation (when the error term for the previous period is correlated with the error term from the current period). Thus, as with any model, the specification is suggested to conduct some form of sensitivity analysis to test a range of model assumptions such as different lags or by employing methods to control for potential biases from such factors as serial autocorrelation.

Going back to our example of dental caries in children after the introduction of a sugar tax, a basic model specification would like something like:

$$DC_{it} = \beta_0 + \beta_1 X_{\mathrm{pre}} + \beta_2 X_{\mathrm{post}} + \varepsilon_{it},$$

where DC is a continuous variable for amount of dental caries. β_0 is the intercept or the mean number of dental caries for the sample population if there were no other controls in the model. Looking at the intercept is a good way to get a sense check if the regression model looks sensible in linear regression models. If the intercept is far from the mean then the model may be misspecified. β_1 is the baseline trend in dental caries in children and X_{pre} is a vector containing child characteristics variables such as socioeconomic status and sugar consumption. This captures the trend in dental caries before the introduction of the sugar tax. β_2 is the trend change after the introduction of the sugar tax and X_{post} is a vector containing child characteristics after the introduction of the sugar tax. When entering your regression equation in a statistical software package, you need to make sure the programme can control for the policy change. To do this you need to make sure the data is clearly divided by pre- and post-policy period.

Interpreting Results from ITS

Amount of dental caries	Coefficient	95% confidence intervals
Intercept β_0	0.98	0.23–0.89
Baseline trend β_1	1.27	1.06–3.75
Trend change after introduction of sugar tax β_2	0.67	0.13–0.78
Hypothetical results not based on real data		

From the results above, we can see that the mean amount of dental cavities in children is approximately 1. The baseline trend is approximately 1.27 cavities conditional on child characteristics. After the introduction of the sugar tax there is a fall in the mean amount of dental cavities in children to just under 1 (0.67). From this hypothetical data we could draw the conclusion that the sugar tax reduces the mean number of dental cavities in children.

Regression Discontinuity Approach

The RD approach is used on non-experimental observational data where treatment is observed according to whether an observed 'assignment' variable (i.e. a clear indicator that an individual received treatment) exceeds a known cut-off point. An example may make it clearer. Say the local clinical commissioning group (CCG) decides to offer free gym membership to all those who are classified as obese by BMI to try and reduce the number of obese individuals developing diabetes. To evaluate the success of this initiative you could look at the BMI of individuals who just missed receiving the treatment (i.e. those with a BMI of 28 kg/m^2 and 29 kg/m^2 compared with those with a BMI of 30 kg/m^2 or just over, to determine if free gym membership reduced the likelihood of developing diabetes.

When to Use RD

RD is used when researchers are interested in the causal outcome of a binary intervention or treatment (Imbens and Lemieux 2008). The effect of the treatment may be heterogeneous between individuals. There are two main types of RD design: sharp (SRD) and fuzzy (FRD). SRD is used when all individuals eligible for the treatment need to take the treatment. FRD is when not all eligible participants take the treatment but there is an added incentive for them to do so. I will clarify this with an example using two slightly different interventions aimed at reducing the risk of type 2 diabetes. An intervention that could be evaluated using a SRD approach would be a school-based intervention targeting all children who were classified as overweight to participate in an additional hour of physical education at school each week. As all children classified as overweight would be required to participate, then you could evaluate if the intervention reduced the risk of developing type 2 diabetes by comparing the incidence of new cases of type 2 diabetes between those children who are on the edge of being classified as overweight with those who are just below the cut off. Graphically this is shown in Fig. 5.2.

An example of a type 2 diabetes intervention where you would use an FRD would be if a prescription of free gym membership was offered to individuals living in a CCG with a BMI of greater than 30 kg/m^2. The free gym membership would be an incentive to participate in more physical activity, but there is no mandatory requirement for these individuals to use it. We can therefore use an FRD to estimate the causal impact of free gym membership between those who are classified as obese and those with a BMI of 28 kg/m^2 and 29 kg/m^2, controlling for the fact that not everyone who is prescribed free gym membership will use it. This is shown graphically in Fig. 5.3.

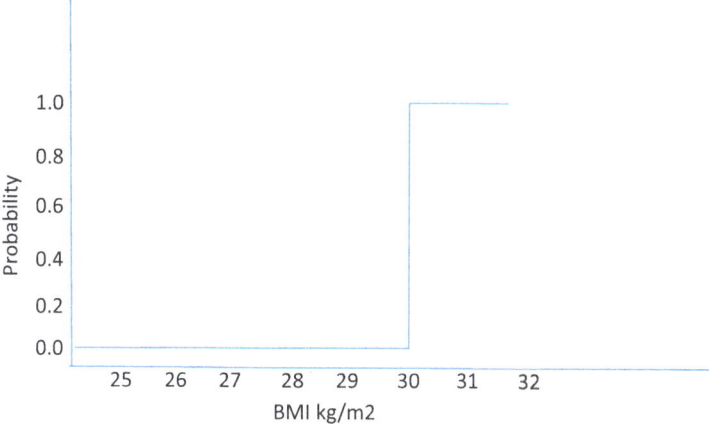

Fig. 5.2 Assignment probabilities for SRD

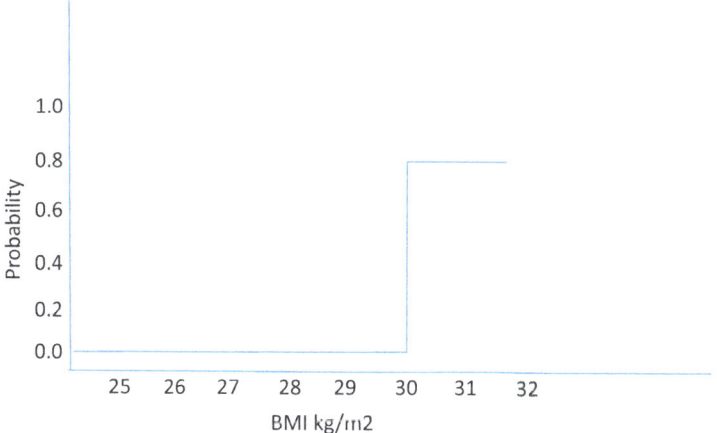

Fig. 5.3 Assignment probabilities for FRD

How to Use RD

Let Diabetes$_i$(0) and Diabetes$_i$(1) denote the potential outcomes for an individual (i). Using the example discussed above this would be the likelihood of developing type 2 diabetes. Diabetes$_i$(0) is the outcome if they were not exposed to the intervention (did not receive free gym membership) and Diabetes$_i$(1) is the outcome if they were exposed to the intervention (did receive free gym membership). To determine the impact of the intervention we want to know the difference between Diabetes$_i$(1) and Diabetes$_i$(0). As we cannot observe this for a single individual we need to focus on the average effects of the treatment; that is, the population average of Diabetes(1) − Diabetes(0).

For each individual i we observe if the outcome corresponding to the treatment received. To formally show this, let $T_i \in \{0, 1\}$ denote the treatment received with $T_i = 0$ if the individual was not exposed to the treatment (did not receive free gym membership) and $T_i = 1$ if the individual did receive the treatment (did receive free gym membership). The observed outcome can then be written as:

$$Y_i = \left(1 - T_i\right)\text{Diabetes}_i\left(0\right) + T_i\,\text{Diabetes}_i\left(1\right) = \begin{cases} \text{Diabetes}_i\left(0\right) & \text{if}\,T_i = 0, \\ \text{Diabetes}_i\left(1\right) & \text{if}\,T_i = 1 \end{cases}$$

In addition to assignment to the treatment, we also need information on covariates or pre-treatment variables which can formally be presented as (Z_i) and which should not be directly affected by the treatment (i.e. characteristics such as age, gender, childhood socioeconomic status, family history of type 2 diabetes).

The key assumption for RD is that we also observe an identifying variable X_i, which determines an individual's treatment status being on either side of a fixed threshold. In our example, this would be an individual's BMI being above 30 kg/m². This predictor variable may be associated with the potential outcome (risk of developing diabetes), but this association is assumed to be smooth. In plain English, the factors determine the risk of developing type 2 diabetes cannot jump at the cut-off of the intervention because then we cannot identify the causal effect of the intervention. If this holds, then we can say that any discontinuity in the conditional distribution of the outcome (risk of developing type 2 diabetes) as a function of the BMI cut-off of 30 kg/m² is interpreted as evidence of a casual effect of free gym membership (Imbens and Lemieux 2008).

For each individual, we need to observe (Diabetes$_i$, W_i, X_i, and Z_i), which we assume is a random sample from a well-defined population.

This then leads us to how to distinguish between the different types of RD models, SRD and FD, during estimation.

In a SRD, the assignment T_i is a deterministic function of the treatment determining variable X:

$$T_i = 1\{X_i \geq c)$$

All individuals with a covariate value of at least c (in our example this would be a BMI of 30 kg/m^2 or greater) are assigned to the participation group, and it is assumed that participation is mandatory. All individuals with a covariate of less than c are assigned to the treatment group and are not eligible for treatment. Therefore, in the SRD we look at discontinuity in the conditional expectation of the outcome given the covariate to uncover an average causal effect of the treatment (Imbens and Lemieux 2008):

$$\lim_{x \downarrow c} E\left[\text{Diabetes}_i | X_i = x\right] - \lim_{x \uparrow c} E\left[\text{Diabetes}_i | X_i = x\right]$$

Which is interpreted as the average causal effect of the treatment at the discontinuity point:

$$\tau SRD = E\left[\text{Diabetes}_i(1) - \text{Diabetes}_i(0) | X_i = c\right]$$
$$= E\left[\text{Diabetes}(1) | X = c\right] - E\left[\text{Diabetes}(0) | X = c\right]$$

Because of the design of the natural experiment there are no individuals where $X_i = c$ for whom we would observe Diabetes(0), as all individuals where $X_i = c$ would be required to participate in the additional hour of weekly physical activity. In the simplest case, this can be estimated using a simple logit model:

$$\text{Diabetes}_i = \alpha + \tau SRD + X_i \beta + \varepsilon,$$

where Diabetes$_i$ is a binary variable which equals one if individual (i) is observed to have diabetes and is equal to zero otherwise: α is the intercept, SRD is the cut off for the individual being eligible for the intervention with the associated parameter of coefficients, τ. X_i are individual socioeconomic and demographic characteristics that are related to diabetes risk, and ε is the standard error term. Typically, the results are presented in graphical form to ease interpretation.

To interpret Fig. 5.4, we need to be fairly sure that the factors influencing the risk of type 2 diabetes do not abruptly change around a BMI of 30 kg/m^2. If we are fairly sure of this, then we can say that 'B' in Fig. 5.4 would be a reasonable guess for an individual's diabetes risk given that they had received the treatment. 'A' would then be a reasonable guess of an individual's diabetes risk given the counterfactual situation where this same individual would not have received the intervention. From this then we could say that the causal effect of the intervention would be B – A (Lee and Lemieux 2010).

In practice there is a limitation on how close you can get to 'c' to analyse data. The narrower the area you focus on in the analysis the fewer data

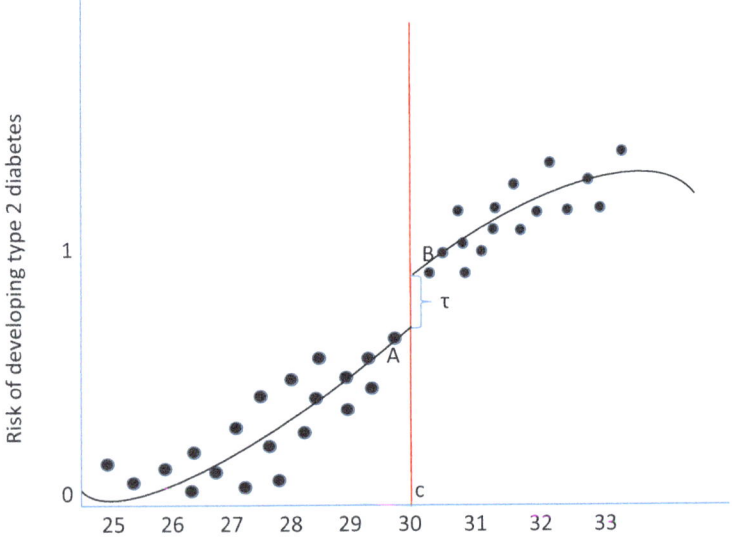

Fig. 5.4   Graphical representation of RD data

there are likely to be. To get a reasonable guess of the treated and untreated states at $X = c$ with finite data, the only option is to use data away from discontinuity (Lee and Lemieux 2010). If the underlying function is truly non-linear, the best unbiased non-linear estimate of τ is the coefficient on SRD. This means that the estimates will be dependent on the chosen functional form of the estimation equation (Lee and Lemieux 2010).

Implementation in Practice

Presenting the results graphically allows you to visually answer the question whether there is evidence of a discontinuity or jump in the outcome at the cut-off point. If there is no evidence of a jump then it is not worthwhile to proceed with further statistical analysis. A graph provides a simple way of visualising the relationship between the outcome and the treatment determining variable. Finally, a graph allows you to check if there is evidence of jumps at any point besides the cut-off. If there are jumps at other points, then there may be other factors instead of the treatment that are affecting the relationship between the outcome variable and determining variable. It is therefore difficult to draw any relationship between the outcome and the intervention. To create a graph like the one in Fig. 5.4, what you need to do is (Jacob et al. 2012):

1. Divide BMI into a number of equal-sized intervals which are often referred to as 'bins' (Jacob et al. 2012). Start defining the bins at the cut-point and work your way to the left and right to ensure that no bins straddle the cut-point (i.e. no bins contain observations from both the control and treatment group). It is difficult to decide the appropriate bandwidth for each bin. The easiest thing to do is try several bandwidths and visually assess which bandwidth makes the graph most informative. The ideal bandwidth is narrow enough so that the patterns in the data are visible especially around the cut-point, but are also wide enough so that noise in the data does not overpower the signal of the data.

2. Calculate the average value of the outcome variable (risk of developing type 2 diabetes) and the midpoint value of the rating variable (BMI) for each bin and count the number of observations in each bin.
3. Plot the average outcome variable for each bin on the Y-axis against the mid-point rating variable for each bin on the X-axis. With our example this means that diabetes risk would be on the Y-axis and BMI would be on the X-axis. The number of observations in each bin can be used as the weight, so that the size of the plotted dot reflects the number of data points in each bin.
4. To help readers better visualise the data, you can superimpose flexible regression lines such as by using the STATA command: *lowess* on top of the plotted data. This also provides a visual description of the amount of noise in the data (Jacob et al. 2012). To ensure robust results, regressions should be estimated separately for observations on the left- and right-hand side of the cut-point.

Generalisability of the Results

Much of the literature argues that the comparison of mean outcomes for participants in the intervention and the control group *only* identifies the mean impact of the programme at values close to the cut point but not across the BMI spectrum. Because of the heterogeneous effects of the intervention, this effect near the cut-off point may be very different to the effect of the intervention away from the cut-off (Jacob et al. 2012).

Fuzzy RD Approach

There are two different types of fuzzy RD designs. In Type 1 fuzzy designs some individuals that are eligible for the treatment do not receive it. These are referred to as 'no-shows'. In Type 2 fuzzy designs some individuals who are eligible for the treatment and some members of the control group receive the treatment. We will focus on Type 1 fuzzy design only.

To give an example, instead of an enforced cut-off for an intervention, such as the one where all schoolchildren are required to do an extra hour of physical activity a week, there may only be a change in the probability of treatment at the cut-off. For example, a prescription for free gym membership for all adults with a BMI of greater than 30 kg/m² does not mean that they will use it (i.e. we may have non-compliers or no shows).

$$\Pr(D_i = 1) = p(V_i)$$

The probability of treatment V_i is a continuous function except at the point at V_0 (where BMI=30 kg/m².

$$\text{Diabetes}_i = f(V_i) + \beta V_i + \varepsilon_i \ (\text{structural equation})$$
$$\text{Diabetes}_i = f(V_i) + \pi_2 1(V_i \geq V_0) + \xi_{2i} \ (\text{reduced form})$$
$$\text{Diabetes}_i = g(V_i) + \pi_1 1(V_i \geq V_0) + \xi_{1i} \ (\text{first stage})$$

The cut-off indicates a change in the probability of receiving treatment (in our case a prescription for free gym membership). Because the treatment may not affect all people with a BMI of greater than 30 kg/m², the jump at the cut-off in the outcomes needs to be rescaled by the jump at the cut-off in the probability of treatment. This is then a standard IV model:

$$\beta = \frac{\pi_2}{\pi_1}$$

Using the IV terminology from Chap. 4, in this case a 'complier' is an individual who takes the treatment when encouraged to do so (i.e. if they are above the threshold and receive the prescription of free gym membership), thereby taking the control of not having gym membership below the threshold.

Graphically the Fuzzy RD design will look similar to that in Fig. 5.4. As an individual's BMI approaches the cut-point then the control and treatment group become increasingly similar, with the exception of the likelihood whether they are offered the treatment. If the risk of developing type 2 diabetes follows a monotonic pattern as BMI increases, then any change of risk at the cut-point would stem from the treatment. Any regression results from a fuzzy RD can be interpreted as LATE or ATE (see description in Chap. 4).

Steps to Estimation

How you go about conducting a RD analysis depends upon whether you are analysing data from a retrospective or a prospective study. A retrospective study is more common. This is when you have the data which lends itself to a RD approach, whereas in a prospective RD study you are collecting data specifically to analyse using a RD approach. These guidelines have been suggested by Jacob et al. (2012):

1. Determine whether you have a valid RD experiment

    (a) Gather all relevant information regarding the process for assigning if an individual is eligible for treatment and how the cut-point is decided and enforced.
    (b) If the design appears to be valid based upon the process used to determine eligibility to the intervention, conduct preliminary graphical and statistical analysis to confirm.

2. Assess whether the design is sharp or fuzzy by determining the probability of receiving the treatment as a function of your deciding variable. (In our example above the deciding variable is BMI.)
3. Determine the degree of precision (this is related to your sample size) you have for detecting impacts. If you have a fuzzy design this needs to be accounted for when assessing precision.
4. Once you are sure that you have chosen the appropriate estimation strategy with sufficient power to detect effects, proceed with the analysis.

(a) Start by graphing the outcome variable versus the determining variable using different bandwidths to smooth the plot. Visually inspect the graph to determine if there is discontinuity at the cut-point.

(b) Estimate your model.

(c) If you have a fuzzy design take this into account when analysing your data.

(d) Unless evidence suggests otherwise, use the simplest model when conducting your analysis. Complex models should be used for sensitivity analysis only.

5. Determine the generalisability of your findings. Think about how much random error may be in the determining variable. For example, is BMI self-reported or nurse assessed? This will provide some insight into how heterogeneous the sample around the cut-point is likely to be. The greater the degree of random error (i.e. not systematic error from people misreporting key variables), the more generalisable your results are likely to be.

If you were to design a study to be analysed using a RD approach, what you would do is:

1. Determine the sample size that you will need to detect effects. Take into account that there are likely to be 'no-shows' that will affect the precision of your results.

2. Work with the implementers of the intervention to ensure that the assignment of treatment will result in data that can be assessed using a RD approach.

3. Monitor the implementation of the intervention to ensure compliance and minimise 'no shows'. Ensure that instances of non-compliance are properly recorded so that they can be controlled for in your analysis.

4. When the intervention is complete, assess the validity of the design using graphical and empirical techniques.

5. Analyse the data using the appropriate regression technique.

6. Assess the generalisability of your findings.

Difference in Difference Approach (DiD)

This approach has stemmed from the idea that a simple pre-post study design may be biased because of unobserved factors (such as drought reducing the amount of Australian wine available, pushing up the price and hence reducing wine consumption by all) that affect outcomes and may also change with the treatment. If these unobserved differences affect the control group as well, then double differencing will remove any bias on the coefficients so that you can isolate the treatment effects.

This approach can be used on data of repeated cross-sections such as the Health Survey of England or longitudinal data such as the Panel Study of Income Dynamics or Understanding Society. It is simplest to present the model if you have outcome data on two groups: one that was impacted by a policy, legislation, or an intervention and another control group that was not. Data is needed for both groups for one period before the intervention/legislation and one period after. If the same individuals within a group are observed in each time period, the average outcome measure in the control group is subtracted from the average outcome measure in the treatment group. Using data from the same individuals over time means that you can control for time unobserved permanent differences between the control and treatment groups that may affect the outcome measure. It also means that you can control for trends over time that may affect the outcome measure for both the treatment and control group (Wooldridge 2007).

Let us make this clearer with an example. Say the Scottish government enacted a minimum price of alcohol and you wanted to compare mean weekly alcohol consumption rates between individuals living in Scotland and those living in England who were not impacted by the legislation. You would need data on similar individuals (based upon socioeconomic status, gender, weekly alcohol consumption before the legislation) living in Scotland and England for one year before the enactment of legislation and one year after the legislation came into force. Some of the unobserved factors that may affect weekly alcohol consumption would be seasonal factors that impact on opportunities to drink, such as the holiday season and enjoyment of drinking alcohol. Trends that may impact on

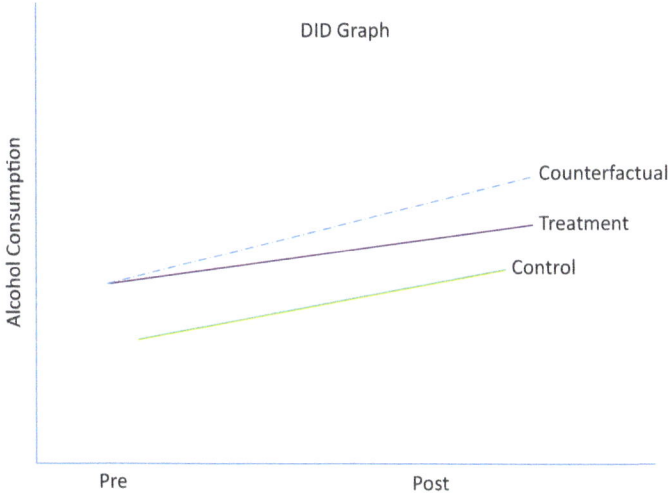

Fig. 5.5 Difference in Difference graph

mean weekly alcohol consumption would be something like a public health information campaign that began before the intervention to get people to reduce their weekly drinking. The set-up can be shown in Fig. 5.5.

The top dotted line in Fig. 5.5 is the counterfactual, which shows what the weekly alcohol consumption would be in Scotland if it had not introduced minimum pricing. The purple treatment line shows the actual alcohol consumption of individuals in Scotland. The green control line shows the weekly alcohol consumption of individuals living in England. For the DiD estimation we will subtract the alcohol consumption of the treatment and control for time unobserved factors that are independent of the control and treatment group, and can be teased out of the coefficients by differencing (similar to the fixed effects model).

Formally, the DiD approach can be shown as (following Wooldridge 2007):

$$Y = \beta_0 + \beta_1 db + \delta_0 d2 + \delta_1 d2\left(db\right) + \varepsilon$$

Using our example, Y would be mean weekly alcohol consumption and $d2$ is a dummy variable for the post-intervention/legislation period. The dummy variable db captures potential differences between the control and treatment group before the intervention/policy change; for example, the propensity to drink or social norms around alcohol consumption which may affect weekly alcohol consumption independent of the policy change. The coefficient of interest is δ_1, which is the parameter of coefficients from $d2 \times db$. This is the same as the dummy variable being equal to one for those who are in the treatment group. The DiD estimator is then:

$$\delta_1 = \left(\bar{Y}_{T2} - \bar{Y}_{T1}\right) - \left(\bar{Y}_{C2} - \bar{Y}_{C1}\right)$$

Inference based upon even modest sample sizes in each of the four groups is relatively straightforward and is robust to using a variety of time periods or different control and treatment groups (Wooldridge 2007).

Because there may be different propensities in alcohol consumption between people in Scotland and England, or a public health information campaign targeted only at individuals living in Scotland, a more robust DiD approach would be to include two control groups in your analysis, one from Scotland (with a subset of the population of legal drinking age) and one from England. Formally this can be shown by:

$$Y = \beta_0 + \beta_1 db + \beta_2 dE + \beta_3 db(dE) + \delta_0 d2 + \delta_1 d2(db) \\ + \delta_2 d2(dE) + \delta_3 d2(db)(dE) + \varepsilon$$

The coefficient of interest in this case is now δ_3, which is the triple interaction term of $d2 \times db \times dE$; this captures differences between the treatment group and the two controls and can be shown as:

$$\hat{\delta}_3 = \left(\bar{Y}_{T2} - \bar{Y}_{T1}\right) - \left(\bar{Y}_{S2} - \bar{Y}_{S1}\right) - \left(\bar{Y}_{C2} - \bar{Y}_{C1}\right),$$

where T, is the treatment group, W is an additional treatment group from Wales, and C is the original control group from England. This estimator is often called the difference in difference in difference (DDD). What this estimation technique does is control for time trend changes in alcohol consumption by using individuals from England as control group and then controls for any changes in alcohol consumption from other related policies by using an additional control group from Scotland.

It is straightforward to add additional covariates to the DiD equation (Wooldridge 2007).

The DD and DDD approach can be applied to data from multiple time periods. To do this the estimation model needs to control for a full set of time dummies. A policy dummy replaces $d2 \times dB$, which is assumed to be unity for groups and time periods after the enactment of the policy. This imposes the restriction that the policy has the same effect each year after it is enacted, but this restriction can be relaxed (Wooldridge 2007). If you are estimating a DDD model with multiple time periods, then the model needs to include a full set of dummies for each of the two types of control groups, all time periods, and all pairwise interactions. A policy dummy/or a continuous variable will then measure the effects of the policy (Wooldridge 2007).

As in the example above, groups are often defined by geography and time period. But this does not necessarily need to be the case. It could also be by socioeconomic status and geography and time or age/gender and geography and time. The most important thing is that differencing is a credible way to deal with non-group equivalence.

Some Things to Keep in Mind

The DiD framework can easily support the addition of time-varying covariates that may impact on the outcome of interest. This will mean more precise standard errors as you will be able to control for more of the factors that impact on your outcome of interest-reducing omitted variable bias in the equation. Similar to the fixed effects model, any covariates that do not vary over time such as gender will be differenced out of the model.

If you are looking at effects over a group such as everyone in Scotland facing the same minimum price for alcohol, then Moulton (1986) and Kloek (1981) show that the standard errors from an OLS equation may be severely biased downwards. Failing to account for the grouped structure can thus lead to incorrect inferences. For fewer than 40 clusters you need to include a different approach to statistical inference. If you have between 40 and 50 clusters, it is possibly that clustering the standard errors may be sufficient to reduce bias, but it may not be. The general opinion is that it is OK as long as data are aggregated to the cell level. For more than 100 clusters you do not have to worry about biased standard errors.

Bootstrapping is one way to get around the cluster standard error problem. The first technique that we can use is the cluster bootstrap. Bootstrapping estimates a model for a specific number of repetitions using samples of the data frame. A simple bootstrap does not necessarily draw from the same observations as it allows for random sampling with replacement. For each repetition the main analysis is repeated on the sample data and the estimates are stored. As soon as all the repetitions are finished, the standard errors are calculated by taking the standard deviation from the stored model estimates. Clustering bootstrapping rather than drawing from observation units with replacements draws from a cluster of units with replacement. To clarify, say that you had data on 1200 individuals from 20 different local authorities; a standard bootstrapping technique would draw 1000 observations from the 1200 individuals where a cluster bootstrap would draw from the 20 local authorities with replacement. As is the case with this example, we have relatively few clusters (20). For this scenario, Cameron and Miller (2015) suggest a 'wild bootstrap procedure'. This method cluster bootstraps the OLS residuals and then generates the finite sample T-test compared to a Wald test for the standard bootstrap technique. Another potential bootstrapping technique is block bootstrapping. With this method the data is divided into several blocks. The accuracy of this technique is sensitive to the choice of block. The optimal block choice depends upon the sample size, the data generating process, and the statistic considered. More information on this method can be found in Hall et al. (1995).

The next step is to ensure that your model is capturing the effects of the intervention. This can be done by re-estimating the equation with placebo checks using periods where the policy or intervention was not in place.

Another issue to be aware of is the problem of Ashenfelter's Dip where there is a dip in intervention participants' outcomes directly after the intervention usually stemming from individual transitory shocks on past outcomes. This may partially result from self-selection into the intervention programme. For example, say you wanted to use a DiD approach to evaluate the impact of a weight loss intervention. Those in the treatment group may have gained weight shortly before the intervention knowing that they were going to participate in a weight loss programme. A pre-treatment trend or 'dip' would create bias in your results. To test for pre-treatment effects we can use the leads of treatment rather than the lags of treatment:

$$Y = \beta_0 + \beta_1 db_{t+1} + \delta_0 d2 + \delta_1 d2\left(db_{t+1}\right) + \varepsilon$$

The null hypothesis is that there are no pre-treatment effects. To test the null hypothesis, we need to:

1. Inspect the coefficients on the leads.
2. Plot the coefficients and confidence intervals leading up to after the onset of treatment.
3. Compute an F-test that the leading coefficients are jointly equal to zero. This is sometimes called the modified Granger Causality Test.

Another method for testing the placebo effect involves the permutation and randomisation tests (see for example Rosenbaum 1987). This approach works out the sampling distribution by fitting the data to the placebo tests. The idea behind this is that you loop the data over 'P' permutations, which randomly shuffles the treatment variable. The DiD model is then fitted using the shuffled treatment. The next step is to store these estimates; then you plot the density of the placebo DiD estimates. Finally, you compute p-values and other relevant statistics using the placebo estimates.

We have now completed a whistle-stop tour of three methods for evaluating causal effects using before or after study designs. Some examples of papers using all these techniques follow, hopefully to inspire you and to give you some tips on how to undertake your own estimations.

Empirical Papers Using These Estimation Techniques

Interrupted Time Series:

Walley, A. Y., Xuan, Z., Hackman, H. H., Quinn, E., Doe-Simkins, M., Sorensen-Alawad, A., … Ozonoff, A. (2013). Opioid overdose rates and implementation of overdose education and nasal naloxone distribution in Massachusetts: Interrupted time series analysis. *BMJ, 346,* f174.
Lopez Bernal, J. A., Gasparrini, A., Artundo, C. M., & McKee, M. (2013). The effect of the late 2000s financial crisis on suicides in Spain: An interrupted time-series analysis. *The European Journal of Public Health, 23*(5), 732–736.
Pridemore, W. A., & Snowden, A. J. (2009). Reduction in suicide mortality following a new national alcohol policy in Slovenia: An interrupted time-series analysis. *American Journal of Public Health, 99*(5), 915–920.

Regression Discontinuity Approach:

Ludwig, J., & Miller, D. L. (2007). Does head start improve children's life chances? Evidence from a regression discontinuity design. *The Quarterly Journal of Economics, 122*(1), 159–208.
McEwan, P. J. (2013). The impact of Chile's school feeding program on education outcomes. *Economics of Education Review, 32,* 122–139.
Andalón, M. (2011). Oportunidades to reduce overweight and obesity in Mexico? *Health Economics, 20*(S1), 1–18.

Questions to Consider

1. You have data on two local authorities over a four-year period, where in the third year of that data an intervention providing free healthy snacks to children in primary school was implemented. You want to know if giving children healthy snacks impacted on their academic performance. Which would be the most appropriate evaluation technique to use to estimate a causal effect of healthy snacks on academic performance?
2. A new programme helped people with chronic conditions return to work. All individuals with at least one chronic condition who were out of work qualify for a return to work training scheme. What evaluation technique would you use to determine if this training scheme was causally associated with an increase in employment rates?
3. New legislation came into force which stopped hospitals from selling junk food. What evaluation technique would you use to determine if this impacted on patient outcomes? What sort of data would you need to address this evaluation question?

References and Further Reading

Interrupted Time Series

Bernal, J. L., Cummins, S., & Gasparrini, A. (2017). Interrupted time series regression for the evaluation of public health interventions: A tutorial. *International Journal of Epidemiology, 46*(1), 348–355.

Kontopantelis, E., Doran, T., Springate, D. A., Buchan, I., & Reeves, D. (2015). Regression based quasi-experimental approach when randomisation is not an option: Interrupted time series analysis. *BMJ, 350*, h2750.

Regression Discontinuity

Imbens, G. W., & Lemieux, T. (2008). Regression discontinuity designs: A guide to practice. *Journal of Econometrics, 142*(2), 615–635.

Jacob, R., Zhu, P., Somers, M. A., & Bloom, H. (2012). *A practical guide to regression discontinuity.* MDRC.

Lee, D. S., & Lemieux, T. (2010). Regression discontinuity designs in economics. *Journal of Economic Literature, 48*, 281–355.

Difference in Difference

Cameron, A. C., & Miller, D. L. (2015). A practitioner's guide to cluster-robust inference. *Journal of Human Resources, 50*(2), 317–372.

Hall, P., Horowitz, J. L., & Jing, B. Y. (1995). On blocking rules for the bootstrap with dependent data. *Biometrika, 82*(3), 561–574.

Heckman, J. J., & Smith, J. A. (1999). The pre-programme earnings dip and the determinants of participation in a social programme. Implications for simple programme evaluation strategies. *The Economic Journal, 109*(457), 313–348.

Kloek, T. (1981). OLS estimation in a model where a microvariable is explained by aggregates and contemporaneous disturbances are equicorrelated. *Econometrica: Journal of the Econometric Society, 49*(1), 205–207.

Moulton, B. R. (1986). Random group effects and the precision of regression estimates. *Journal of Econometrics, 32*(3), 385–397.

Rosenbaum, P. R. (1987). Sensitivity analysis for certain permutation inferences in matched observational studies. *Biometrika, 74*(1), 13–26.

Wooldridge, J. (2007). What's new in econometrics? Lecture 10 difference-in-differences estimation. NBER Summer Institute. Retrieved October 9, 2017, from www.nber.org/WNE/Slides7–31–07/slides_10_diffindiffs.pdf

6

Cross-Country Comparisons

Learning Outcomes:

* Identify how cross-country analysis can be used for public health policy making
* Identify an evaluation technique that can be used for cross-country analysis of public health issues
* Discuss the strengths and weaknesses of cross-country analysis

All health care systems in high income countries (HICs) face similar pressures related to improving efficiency, patient care, and limited funding. A scarcity of resources means that decision makers need to choose what is funded. For example, should the health care system focus on prevention or treatment, or a mixture of the two? What is the optimal mixture? There is also continuing pressure on health care professionals to improve patient experience and patient care. This needs to be considered in the matrix of limited resources. How can patient care be improved without reducing the number of services available? In addition, there are a number of demographic pressures facing HICs. There is the rising number of people suffering from non-communicable dis-

© The Author(s) 2018
H. Brown, *The Economics of Public Health*,
https://doi.org/10.1007/978-3-319-74826-9_6

eases such as diabetes, heart disease from sedentary lifestyles, and rising obesity rates in conjunction with an ageing population. This puts pressure on the existing resources of health care systems. Finally, external economic factors need to be thrown into this mix. Events such as the 2008 financial crisis impacted on government budgets and the total amount of money available for health. Economic recessions also impact on individual health, increasing levels of mental health problems, alcohol and drug misuse, and suicides (see for example Bor et al. 2013;Gili et al. 2012; Reeves et al. 2012), putting further pressure on health care systems.

So where does this leave us? Given the challenges faced by all HICs, cross-country comparisons provide a good opportunity to evaluate a country-specific response to these challenges to identify if it is having the intended consequences. It is an opportunity for countries to identify good practice as well as learn from each other's mistakes so that they are not repeated again. In addition, as illustrated in Fig. 6.1, which shows

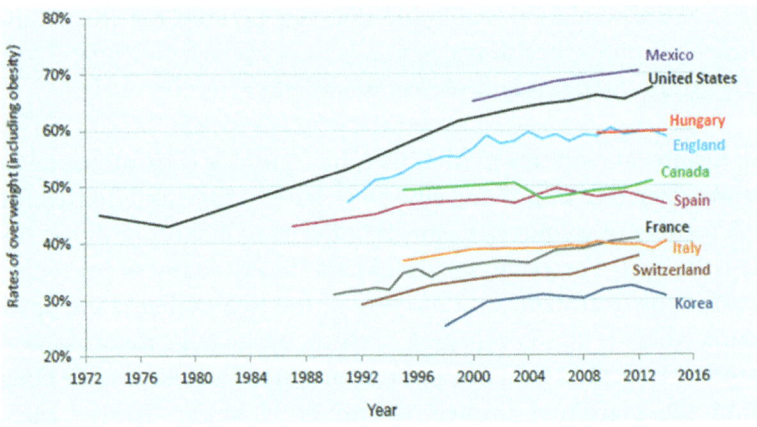

Fig. 6.1 Rising overweight (including obesity) rates in adults aged 15–74 years. Note: Overweight and obesity rates designate overweight and obesity prevalence rates. Age and gender adjusted rates of overweight (including obesity), using the 2005 OECD standard population. Measured height and weight in England, Hungary, Korea, Mexico, and the USA; self-reported in other countries. Source: OECD analysis of health survey data

obesity rates in a number of countries, cross-country analysis can be used to assess how worse or best case scenarios in terms of obesity rates would impact on the provision of health care services.

How to Conduct Cross-Country Analysis

The first step is identifying your research question. Is there a specific aspect of health care delivery/policy that can best be addressed by comparing outcomes between two or more countries? For example, say you were interested in the relationship between sickness payment and return to work rates. Cross-country analysis could potentially be used to compare how different rates of sickness payment offered by different countries impact on return to work rates. Alternatively, if you were planning your budget around preventative health care measures related to obesity, you would possibly want to compare obesity preventative policies with countries that had similar rates of obesity and those with higher and lower rates to try and project future need. Cross-country analysis could also be used to explore mental health outcomes in retired individuals. This list is not conclusive, and simply identifies a few areas where cross-country analysis could be used.

Identifying Data Sources

In Chap. 3, we identified a number of data sources that can be used for analysis. When doing cross-country analysis there is an extra layer of complication to choosing appropriate datasets: you need to choose data that can be compared between countries. Many of the large household surveys such as the Understanding Society Survey and its predecessor the British Household Panel Survey, the German Socioeconomic Panel, and the Household Income and Dynamic Survey of Australia have all been designed to be comparable with the Panel Study of Income Dynamics (the first continuous longitudinal household survey in the world, which began in 1968 in the USA). Other datasets, such as SHARE (also mentioned in Chap. 3), have been specifically designed for cross-country analysis between European countries. Similarly, for looking at macro-level factors, OECD has been specifically designed for cross-country analysis. The purveyors of these datasets have already ensured that the variables have been equivalised so that cross-country analysis can be easily performed.

Many of the large household surveys such as the ones mentioned above ask respondents similar questions, which in theory can be used for cross-country analysis. However, it is important to keep in mind that how people respond to these questions may differ between countries. It is possible that methods to control for individual heterogeneity when using data from within one country, such as generalised least squares or fixed effects methods, can control for this type of interpretation. There may also be different social norms associated with claiming sickness benefits. If you assume that these norms are unobserved and relatively constant over time, then this can also be controlled for in traditional ways in cross-country analysis, such as a fixed effects or proxy fixed effects approach.

However, if individuals are claiming sickness benefits they may be more inclined to report worse health and associated outcomes to justify their receipt of the benefit, and this could bias the analysis. Sickness benefits will not be the same in all your countries of analysis, and if health reporting in some of your data is related to sickness benefits then your results will be biased.

All this highlights the important of context and the research question. What you have to do is identify the relevant questions from each of the surveys you plan on using for your cross-country analysis. Next, you have to decide what type of bias may impact on the hypothesised relationship. This will determine what the most appropriate analysis technique will be.

Analysis Method

A good first step would be to try all analysis using a simple estimation approach such as OLS on data from each individual country and compare results between countries. The next step would be to identify what type of bias may impact on your results. Some things to consider when doing cross-country analysis are the underlying trends that affect the relationship you are interested in. Because of differing economic conditions, cultural and social norms, and designs of health care systems it is likely that many underlying trends related to public health issues could be different. If you find evidence of difference in underlying trends, then a difference in difference approach would not be appropriate.

For public health issues, trends may be similar between countries, as can be seen with the obesity figure above; it looks as if many countries are on similar upward obesity trajectories. If you are fairly confident that any of the potential bias affecting your data stems from factors that can be generalisable across countries and is not likely to be country and more specifically research question specific, then there are numerous different ways to analyse the data.

In this chapter, we will introduce one new estimation technique, *propensity score matching* (PSM).

The Example

Suppose you were interested in understanding the relationship between a statutory retirement age and mental well-being in older adults. A PSM approach means you match individuals from different countries, some with a statutory retirement age and others without, in order to try and identify the role of a statutory retirement age on mental well-being in older adults.

Propensity Score Matching in Cross-Country Analysis

PSM is another analysis technique where observational data is organised in a quasi-experimental framework to estimate the causal effects of a policy. The propensity score is a probability that certain characteristics influence the likelihood of being assigned to the treatment rather than the control group. These scores then reduce selection bias by weighting the observable characteristics of individuals in the treatment and control group. If omitted variable bias such as this is biasing the results from OLS coefficients, meaning you cannot estimate causal effects, a PSM approach may be able to reduce this bias.

When to Use PSM

PSM is usually used when either randomisation, other quasi-experimental approaches such as RD, ITS, etc. are not possible given the research question or available data. Why would you want to use PSM for cross-country analysis? This approach can be used to highlight how system-level differences such as sickness payment levels, or an aspect of the design of the health care system, such as copayment, may impact on outcomes. It is important if you are using PSM for cross-country analysis that besides these system-level factors, which are of interest for your research question, other important characteristics are similar between the countries you are interested in. Examples are similar macroeconomic conditions or distribution of occupations across the socioeconomic spectrum.

Matching

In order for PSM to be an appropriate method, the most important thing is to choose an appropriate comparison group. Matches are usually based upon 'pre-treatment' characteristics to avoid bias from the treatment impacting on the results. In our example of a statutory retirement age, if the retirement age was 65 then it would be sensible to match individuals at age 60 to reduce bias from expectations around an impending retirement changing behaviour. Matches are based on observable characteristics such as age, gender, occupation, and educational attainment. When using this approach we assume that there are no significant differences between the treatment and control group based upon unobservable characteristics, say for example a desire to continue working into older age. All key differences between groups must be in the data for PSM to produce unbiased results.

PSM matches those in the treatment and control groups on the estimate probability of being treated. In our example, this means matching those in a country with a statutory retirement age (treatment) to those living in a country without a statutory retirement age (control). In its simplest form the idea of matching can be shown as:

$$P(X) = \Pr(d = 1 | X)$$

Let X be individual characteristics. In this case D would indicate living in a country with a statutory retirement age. Instead of creating an exact match for each participation by X, we can instead match on the probability of D (living in a country with statutory retirement age).

A key assumption of the model is that participation is independent of the outcome conditional on X_i:

$$E\left[y_0 \,|\, X, d = 1\right] = E\left[y_0 \,|\, X, d = 0\right]$$

This would not hold true if there were unobserved factors impacting on d. In our example this is not likely to be the case, as it does not seem realistic that individuals would move to a different country specifically because of a statutory retirement age.

This assumption not only permits matching at the mean but also balances the distribution of observed characteristics between the treatment and control group.

Figure 6.2 illustrates the matching process. Each individual in the treatment group is paired to some group of comparable 'non-treated' individuals. As shown in Fig. 6.2, the next step is to find the region of common support that is the weighted outcome of the 'treated' individuals with those of their 'neighbours' in the comparison group.

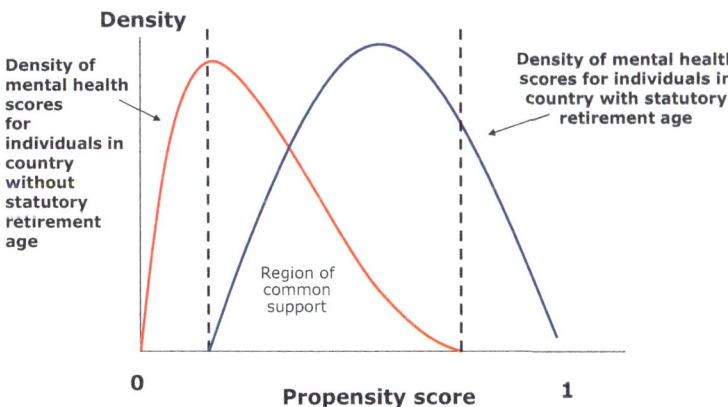

Fig. 6.2 Propensity score matching

There are two broad groups of matching estimators: individual neighbourhood and weights. Individual matching is a one-to-one match of the control and treatment group. There are a number of different individual matching techniques:

1. Nearest neighbour: An individual in the treatment group i is matched to an individual in the non-treated group j so that:

$$\left| p_i - p_j \right| = \min_{k \in \{D=0\}} \left\{ p_i - p_k \right\},$$

where $k = j$.

2. Caliper matching: For a pre-specified maximum tolerated difference between the treatment and control group (specified as a standard deviation) which we will refer to as $\delta > 0$, a treated individual i, is matched to a non-treated individual j such that:

$$\delta > \left| p_i - p_j \right| = \min_{k \in \{D=0\}} \left\{ p_i - p_k \right\}$$

If none of the non-treated individuals is within δ standard deviations of a treated individual, this individual from the treated group is left unmatched.

For weighted matching the weighted average outcome of a percentage could be all individuals in the non-treated group. The weight given to non-treated individuals j is in proportion to the closeness of observable characteristics in the treatment and non-treatment group.

1. *Kernel-based matching*: With this approach, the outcome (in our case mental health) of individuals in the treatment group is matched with the kernel-weighted outcome of all individuals in the non-treated group. The weight given to the non-treated individual represented by j is in proportion to the closeness between i and j.

2. *Mahalanobis metric matching*: This technique aims to control for differences due to X by choosing a sub-sample G_2 that tries to match the distributions in the final sample by a random order nearest neighbour. To do this, randomly order the G_1 individuals, then choose for each G_1 unit the nearest available and previously unmatched non-treated individual as a match. The nearest is defined by the sample Mahalanobis Metric. In other words, let X_1 and X_2 be the values of X for individuals G_1 and G_2. Then the distance between the individuals is:

$$\left(X_1 - X_2\right)S^{-1}\left(X_1 - X_2\right)^T,$$

where $S = \{(N-1)S_1 + (rN-1)S_2/(N + rN - 2)$.
In this scenario, S_i is the sample variance of X in G_i where $i = 1, 2$. The resulting matched sample will have N pairs of G_1–G_2 individuals 'close' with respect to the matching variable X (Rubin 1980).

How to Implement in Practice

The data for the treated and non-treated group need to be representative and comparable. This may be more of a challenge if doing cross-country comparison. It is important to ensure that the variables that you plan on using for the analysis are measuring the same thing. If there any cross-country differences in how people may respond to key variables, you need to understand what these are and how they may bias the data. Thinking of the mental health example, if there are cross-country differences in how people report mental health because of cultural or social norms or access to early retirement from mental health issues, this could bias your analysis of the role of statutory retirement age on mental health in older individuals. If this bias is likely to work in a consistent way, it is possible to control for it using a variant of the PSM approach, which we will discuss in greater detail in the next section.

Once you are convinced that you have appropriate data, the next step will be to use a binary nonlinear model such as a probit or a logit to estimate the likelihood of retirement (for our example) given a set of observable characteristics. The predicted values from this binary non-linear model to generate propensity scores $p(x_i)$ for all treated and non-treated individuals.

For each matched pair restrict the sample to a common support as illustrated in Fig. 6.2 using one of the matching techniques described above (caliper, nearest neighbour, etc.). This involves determining a tolerance level for matches which is dependent on the type of matching you choose. How different can individuals in the control and treatment be and still be classified as a match? Once you are satisfied that you have chosen an appropriate matching technique, you can calculate the impact of the policy/legislation by comparing the mean outcomes (mental health scores) between the treated and non-treated group. If PSM addresses the type of bias that was impacting on results from a simple OLS model, then your results will tell you the causal impact of statutory retirement on mental health in older individuals.

It is preferable to match on pre-intervention policy data to ensure that the intervention has not changed key characteristics leading to endogeneity bias. If these data are not available it is possible to match on post-intervention characteristics, but you need to be certain that they could not have changed because of the intervention; for example, characteristics such as age and gender. It is important to remember that matching only controls for observable differences but cannot control for unobservable differences.

PSM requires large samples and good data that do not suffer from data input errors, and where the administrators of the data have taken steps to reduce measurement error by psychometric testing of questions or through the use of internationally validated measures. It is important that unless the area that you are looking at is impact of access to a particular service or an institutional factor, such as sickness payments, that the treated and non-treated group have access to similar institutions and market factors such as employment trends. The data must also include a range of variables that can be used to identify treatment status and outcomes.

Some Extensions

It is important to remember that PSM as a stand-alone estimation technique can only control for observable differences between the treated and non-treated group. If there are unobservable differences these can bias your results and limit your ability to estimate a causal impact of a policy/intervention. Because of this limitation of PSM it is sensible to try and use a dual estimation approach which combines PSM with an additional estimation technique.

Going back to our example, if you thought there were time constant unobserved factors that may impact on mental health in older adults then PSM could be linked with a difference in difference estimation approach. This would remove the bias from time constant unobserved trends impacting on outcomes in the treated and non-treated groups. This means that you are able to control for some of the unobserved bias that may be impacting on your coefficients. As was mentioned in Chap. 5 (see Fig. 5.5), this relies upon similar underlying trends being present in your treated and non-treated groups. To employ this estimation approach you will require panel data, or if you are investigating impacts at the population level a repeated cross-section.

If you think there may be unobserved differences between the treated and non-treated group but a difference in underlying trends, an alternative approach would be to add as an additional explanatory variable the lagged dependent variable (O'Neill et al. 2016). Again, this would require panel data.

Interpretation of Coefficients

Results can be interpreted as either Average Treatment Effect (ATE) or Average Treatment Effect on the Treated (ATET). ATET estimates the mean difference between the treated and non-treated groups. The only required assumption relates to the ability to identify potential outcomes of comparable individuals in the non-treated group to estimate counterfactuals:

$$L_0 \perp T \,|\, X \tag{6.1}$$

which implies that:

$$E\left(L_0 | T = 1, X\right) - E\left(L_0 | T = 0, X\right) = 0 \tag{6.2}$$

To identify the ATET, we need to assume the common support condition that for each treated individual there are control individuals with the same X:

$$P\left(T = 1|X\right) < 1 \qquad (6.3)$$

Utilising the assumptions from Eqs. 6.1 and 6.3 we can estimate the ATET from the difference in outcomes between the treatment and controls within each cell defined by the condition variables X (Blundell and Costa Dias 2009).

Employing the law of iterated expectations and the selection on observables assumption, the ATET can be obtained from observational data by:

$$\text{ATET} = \begin{cases} E\left(L_1|T = 1\right) - E\left(L_0|T = 0\right) \\ E_x\left[\left(E\left(L_1|X,T = 1\right) - \left(E\left(L_0|X,T = 1\right)\right)\right) + T = 1\right] \\ E_x\left[\left(E\left(L_1|X,T = 1\right) - \left(E\left(L_0|X,T = 0\right)\right)\right) + T = 1\right] \end{cases} \quad (6.4)$$

This is too restrictive when the set of conditioning variables is large, so instead we condition on the probability of treatment as a function of X the propensity score $P(X)$. After the propensity score is estimated, we estimate the ATET by reweighting on the propensity score (Cerulli 2013).

ATE shows the mean effects across the whole population. For further information see the discussion in Chap. 3 for interpretation of IV results.

A Further Example

How does the diagnosis of a chronic condition such as depression, chronic obstructive pulmonary disease COPD, or diabetes impact on employment and wages? Why would this research question best be answered by comparing outcomes across countries? It is possible that there are system-level factors such as the generosity and accessibility of the welfare system and employment legislation that may impact on an individual's attachment to the labour market after the diagnosis of a chronic condition. If you were to perform the analysis in only one country, you might miss these factors. For illustrative purposes, we will show an analysis using PSM for one country.

Data

The analysis will use five years of data (2009–2014) of the Understanding Society Survey (University of Essex 2016). The key health variables that we are interested in are a diagnosis of cancer, diabetes, depression, or COPD between the current period t and the previous period $t-1$. The key employment variables we are interested in are employment status, which will be measured as a binary variable if an individual reports either being employed or self-employed, and log of hourly wage. The additional controls that we will want to match on are educational attainment, age, gender, marital status, number of dependent children under the age of 12, region, a binary indicator for living in an urban or rural area, gender, firm size, and occupation. In this example, in the base period we will want everyone to be working before a diagnosis of a chronic condition. This is to ensure that the control and treatment group are as similar to each other as possible. The treatment and control group will be discussed in more detail below.

Constructing Treated and Non-Treated Groups

The first thing to do would be to look at previous literature on the topic area. Is there anything that is commonly done? For this research question, there have been a number of studies which have tried to estimate causal effects (García Gómez and López Nicolás 2006; García-Gómez 2011). What we did is use a three-year period ($t = 1$, $t = 2$, and $t = 3$). To be included in the sample an individual must be working in the first period ($t = 1$). The treated group is diagnosed with one of the four chronic conditions (diabetes, cancer, depression, COPD) between period $t = 1$ and

Table 6.1 Baseline descriptive statistics

	Chronic condition				
	Treatment		Control		
	$n = 2836$		$n = 19,642$		p-value
	Mean	S.D.	Mean	S.D.	(diff)
Female	**0.61**	**0.49**	**0.51**	**0.50**	**0.001**
Age	**44.38**	**10.96**	**40.84**	**11.41**	**0.001**
Degree	0.47	0.50	0.47	0.50	0.92
A-Level	0.23	0.42	0.24	0.43	0.21
GCSE	0.23	0.42	0.23	0.42	0.81
Married	0.57	0.50	0.57	0.50	0.94
Divorced/separated	**0.16**	**0.37**	**0.11**	**0.32**	**0.001**
Widowed	0.02	0.14	0.01	0.10	0.48
Kids under 12	**0.28**	**0.45**	**0.34**	**0.47**	**0.001**
Annual income	18,660	13,979	18,938	14,010	0.32
Hourly wage	**11.15**	**8.26**	**12.23**	**9.16**	**0.00**
Firm size	0.67	0.47	0.68	0.46	0.16
Urban	0.76	0.43	0.75	0.43	0.59
Region	**5.28**	**3.33**	**5.51**	**3.43**	**0.001**
Professionals	0.06	0.24	0.06	0.25	0.76
Intermediate workers	0.25	0.43	0.24	0.43	0.40
Small employers	0.11	0.32	0.11	0.32	1.00
Lower supervisory/tech	0.30	0.46	0.31	0.46	0.56
Semi-routine	0.10	0.31	0.09	0.28	0.25
Routine	0.04	0.19	0.04	0.19	0.95

Notes: Variables in bold indicate statistically significantly different at $p < 0.05$

$t = 2$ or between period $t = 2$ and $t = 3$. The non-treated group (i.e. control) is not diagnosed with one of these four conditions between period $t = 1$ and $t = 2$ or between period $t = 2$ and $t = 3$.

As can be seen in Table 6.1, there are some differences between the treated and non-treated groups in terms of the percentage of women, with significantly more women suffering from one of the four chronic conditions during this period. Additionally, those in the treatment groups are older, have a mean log of hourly wage before their diagnosis, are more likely to be divorced or separated, are less likely to have dependent children under the age of 12, and live in a different geographic region in the UK.

The first step is to estimate a simple probit model.

Table 6.2 Marginal effects of likelihood of remaining in employment for four conditions

	Men	Women
Cancer no hospital	−0.23***	0.20***
Cancer hospital	−1.71***	−0.51***
COPD no hospital	−0.19***	0.45***
COPD hospital	−1.94***	−1.62***
Diabetes no hospital	−0.61***	−0.69***
Diabetes hospital	0.77***	−1.61***
Depression no hospital	−0.94***	−0.71***
Depression hospital	−2.82***	−2.19***
n	2442	2983

Note: *** indicates significant at the 1% level
No hospital is individuals diagnosed with condition but no hospital stay compared with those not diagnosed with condition and no hospital stay
Hospital is individuals diagnosed with new condition who had a hospital stay because of this condition compared with those with no new diagnosis and no hospital stay
Estimated using a random effects probit. Additional controls were marital status, age, age squared, educational attainment, dependent children under 12, urban, and region

The results from Table 6.2 above would suggest that there is a large effect of a diagnosis of one of these four conditions on the likelihood of remaining in employment. This effect is larger for those with a hospital stay.

Next, we investigate how diagnosis of one of the four chronic conditions impacts on hourly wage using a simple regression technique; this is summarised in Table 6.3.

The results in Table 6.3 above suggest that if individuals remain in employment there is not a significant impact of being diagnosed with one of the four chronic conditions on their wages.

The next step is to use a PSM approach to estimate the ATET of being diagnosed with one of the four conditions. The simple analysis in Tables 6.2 and 6.3 suggests that we would really only expect to see a difference in employment, as the chronic conditions are not significant in the wage equations.

Comparing it with the results from Table 6.2, we can see that the coefficients are much smaller in the models in Table 6.4. The only coefficients which are significant in the PSM models are a new diagnosis of depression,

Table 6.3 Marginal effects of hourly wage for four conditions

	Men	Women
Cancer no hospital	0.10	0.09
Cancer hospital	−0.17	0.08
COPD no hospital	−0.02	0.03
COPD hospital	−0.29	−0.21
Diabetes no hospital	−0.10	0.04
Diabetes hospital	−0.19	0.12
Depression no hospital	−0.05	−0.04
Depression hospital	−0.13	−0.03
IMR	−0.84*** (0.13)	0.03 (0.27)
n	1635	2347

Note: *** indicates significant at the 1% level, IMR is Inverse Mills Ratio
No hospital is individuals diagnosed with condition but no hospital stay
  compared with those not diagnosed with condition and no hospital stay
Hospital is individuals diagnosed with new condition who had a hospital stay
  because of this condition compared with those with no new diagnosis and no
  hospital stay
Estimated using a generalised least squares regression. Additional controls were
  age, age squared, educational attainment, urban, region, occupation, and firm
  size. Standard errors are bootstrapped

Table 6.4 Propensity score matching four conditions (employment)

	Men	Women
Cancer	−0.02 (0.02)	0.01 (0.01)
COPD	−0.01 (0.03)	0.004 (0.02)
Diabetes	−0.01 (0.01)	−0.02 (0.02)
Depression	−0.05*** (0.01)	−0.03** (0.01)
n	41,753	47,655

Note: ** indicates significance at the 5% level; *** indicates significant at the
  1% level
Estimated using a probit model. Dependent variable is health outcome.
  Independent variables are marital status, age, age squared, educational
  attainment, dependent children under 12, urban, and region
Treatment and control groups are matched using a nearest neighbour technique
ATET shown

which decreases the likelihood of a man remaining in employment by 5% and a woman remaining in employment by 3%. This compares with the depression coefficients in Table 6.2 of −0.94 and −0.71 for men and women with a new diagnosis of depression and no hospital admission to −2.82 and −2.19 for men and women respectively with a new depression diagnosis who were hospitalised in the previous year for their diagnosis.

Table 6.5 Propensity score matching four conditions

	Men	Women
Cancer	−0.07 (0.04)	−0.01 (0.03)
COPD	−0.02 (0.05)	−0.07 (0.06)
Diabetes	−0.19*** (0.03)	−0.04 (0.04)
Depression	−0.09** (0.03)	−0.08*** (0.02)
n	32,281	39,712

Note: ** indicates significant at the 5% level; *** indicates significant at the 1% level
Estimated using a probit model. Dependent variable is health outcome. Independent variables are age, age squared, educational attainment, urban, region, occupation, and firm size.
Treatment and control groups are matched using a nearest neighbour technique
ATET shown

What all these findings suggest are that there is likely to be selection bias impacting on your results, meaning that estimates from a simple model cannot provide causal estimates.

Finally we will look at the results from the wage equations estimated using a PSM: this is summarised in Table 6.5

Interestingly, when comparing these results with those in Table 6.3, more of the coefficients are now significant, specifically those on diabetes for men and depression for both genders. This may mean that selection bias is impacting on the results in Table 6.3. Alternatively, it could be the case that the PSM model is inconsistent and the findings from Table 6.5 may lead you to make a Type 2 error. This is a difficulty with estimating in practice the more computationally difficult models required to estimate causal effects. It is essential to be sure that you are able to control for different types of bias that may impact on your coefficients, but by controlling for these different types of bias you may be introducing efficiency problems into your model.

Other Methods for Estimating Cross-Country Differences

As mentioned earlier in the chapter, after you have identified the appropriate datasets for your research question the next key thing to consider is what type of bias may impact on your analysis. If it is likely to be omitted variable bias, then a fixed effects approach as discussed in Chap. 4

may be appropriate. If you want to create a natural policy experiment and need to control for pre-intervention characteristics only rather than with matching, then a DiD approach may be useful. An IV approach is an additional method that could be utilised if you can identify a suitable instrument which would be applicable in each country setting. The key thing is to identify the weaknesses of your data and chosen method, and how this may impact on the reliability and interpretation of your results.

Questions to Consider

1. Why would cross-country analysis be useful for researchers interested in public health questions?
2. Identify the type of bias that PSM controls for.
3. Why would you choose to combine PSM with DiD, fixed effects, or a dynamic model when conducting cross-country analysis?

References and Further Reading

Blundell, R., & Dias, M. C. (2009). Alternative approaches to evaluation in empirical microeconomics. *Journal of Human Resources, 44*(3), 565–640.

Bor, J., Basu, S., Coutts, A., McKee, M., & Stuckler, D. (2013). Alcohol use during the great recession of 2008–2009. *Alcohol and Alcoholism, 48*(3), 343–348.

Cerulli, G. (2013, September). TREATREW: A user–written Stata routine for estimating average treatment effects by reweighting on propensity score. In *United Kingdom Stata Users' Group Meetings 2013* (No. 02). Stata Users Group.

García-Gómez, P. (2011). Institutions, health shocks and labour market outcomes across Europe. *Journal of Health Economics, 30*(1), 200–213.

García-Gómez, P. G., & López-Nicolás, A. (2006). Health shocks, employment and income in the Spanish labour market. *Health Economics, 15*(9), 997–1009.

Gili, M., Roca, M., Basu, S., McKee, M., & Stuckler, D. (2012). The mental health risks of economic crisis in Spain: Evidence from primary care centres, 2006 and 2010. *The European Journal of Public Health, 23*(1), 103–108.

O'Neill, S., Kreif, N., Grieve, R., Sutton, M., & Sekhon, J. S. (2016). Estimating causal effects: Considering three alternatives to difference-in-differences estimation. *Health Services and Outcomes Research Methodology, 16*(1–2), 1–21.

Reeves, A., Stuckler, D., McKee, M., Gunnell, D., Chang, S. S., & Basu, S. (2012). Increase in state suicide rates in the USA during economic recession. *The Lancet, 380*(9856), 1813–1814.

Rubin, D. B. (1980). Bias reduction using Mahalanobis-Metric matching. *Biometrics, 36*, 293–298.

University of Essex. *Institute for Social and Economic Research, NatCen Social Research and Kantar Public, [producers]: Understanding Society: Waves 1–6, 2009–2015 [computer file]*, 8th ed. Colchester, Essex: UK Data Service [distributor], November 2016. SN: 6614.

7

A Practitioner's Guide

Learning Outcomes:

* Define quasi-experimental estimation approach
* Identify the steps needed to use secondary data analysis to address public health data
* Discuss how findings from this research can be used in policy and practice

In the final chapter of this book, we present a generalisable checklist which can be used by public health practitioners and researchers who want to use observational data to answer important public health policy questions (Table 7.1).

Define Your Research Question

When conducting research, the most important thing is to define your research question. Examples provided in this book look at areas such as the effectiveness of a given public health policy, understanding the

© The Author(s) 2018
H. Brown, *The Economics of Public Health*,
https://doi.org/10.1007/978-3-319-74826-9_7

Table 7.1 Research checklist

☐ Define Your Research Question.
☐ Identify an Appropriate Dataset(s).
☐ Estimate a simple regression model such as OLS, probit, or logit model.
☐ Think about different types of bias which may be affecting these coefficients
☐ Identify the most important types of bias that may impact on these coefficients that you want to control for.
☐ Choose an appropriate estimation model that controls for the types of bias you identified in the step above.
☐ Compare coefficients between your chosen model and the base case.
☐ Do the coefficients behave in the way you expect?
☐ If not why not? Did you chosen estimation procedure reduce efficiency/introduce additional bias
☐ Interpret your coefficients
☐ What do your findings mean for policy/practice

population that may be affected by a specific public health issue such as wage discrimination for obese individuals, and the impact of current legislation/policy on public health outcomes. We do not explore methods for economic evaluation such as cost benefit analysis or social return on investment which are commonly used for public health policies (see Guiness and Wiseman 2011 for more information in a public health context). The techniques discussed in this book therefore cannot be used to assess if a policy or intervention is cost effective or assess the cost on the public purse of a public health issue, such as discriminating against obese workers.

Identify an Appropriate Dataset

In Chap. 2 we discussed the different type of datasets freely available. For many research questions, there may be a need to link with datasets that have an administrative cost associated with them, such as hospital episode statistics. It can be costly and time consuming to acquire this data, so you need to factor this into the amount of time required to do your research. It is key to remember that you do not want the data available to influence your research question; rather, you should let the research question guide which data you use. A great thing about employing the quasi-experimental techniques that we discuss in this book is that it provides a way to manipulate the data so that you can try and identify outcomes in the absence of a policy change/intervention, teasing out the effects of an intervention/policy without having to run a potentially costly RCT.

Estimate a Simple Regression Model

The most important task is getting a sense of the basic relationships in terms of the direction and significance between your variables of interest. This can be accomplished using a simple multivariate regression approach such as OLS for linear dependent variables or probits or logits for binary dependent variables. This will guide you to understand what type of bias may impact on your results and what type of estimation model would be appropriate to reduce this bias. It will be also a good starting point to compare results with your more complicated estimation models to determine if they make sense, or if a loss of efficiency in the more complicated models reduces any of the gains from removing potential bias that is impacting on your coefficients.

Identify the Most Important Type of Bias that may be Impacting on your Simple Coefficient Estimates and Choose an Appropriate Model

Another important reason for starting simple is that it is likely you will have some idea of how the proposed relationship between your key variables should look and the factors that may influence this relationship. This will help you identify potential bias that could impact on your coefficients, such as endogeneity bias, omitted variable bias, or reverse causality (see Chap. 4 for more information on these types of bias). Understanding the type of bias that may be affecting the results will help you identify the most appropriate estimation technique to try and identify causal effects.

Compare Coefficients Between Chosen Model and Base Model

The next step is to compare coefficients between your chosen model and base model. Do the coefficients change in magnitude and potentially in significance as expected a priori given the type of bias you think could bias your coefficients? If not, why may this be? Did you identify the wrong type of bias on your coefficients? Is there an error with your chosen estimation technique such as choosing inappropriate instruments? Is it worthwhile trying a different estimation technique?

If the coefficients look sensible how does this help you identify causal effects? What can you say about the relationship between the outcome and key explanatory variables? Do the results suggest that the intervention works/does not work, and what does this mean for rolling out the intervention to a larger scale or providing guidance on potential policy?

It is important to make sure that you do not get caught up in the estimation and lose sight of the initial research question because of all the maths. You need to remember that the point of the estimation was to determine if an intervention/policy is effective or if there is a need for policy/intervention because of a given public health problem.

Questions to Consider

1. Outline the steps required to estimate causal relationships
2. Why is it important to compare results from quasi-experimental methods with basic models of correlation?
3. How would you ensure that your findings from a quasi-experimental research approach were fed into policy and practice?

References and Further Reading

Guiness, L., & Wiseman, V. (2011). *Introduction to health economics. Understanding public health* (2nd ed.). Maidenhead: Open University Press.

Index

© The Author(s) 2018
H. Brown, *The Economics of Public Health*,
https://doi.org/10.1007/978-3-319-74826-9

The manufacturer's authorised representative in the EU is Springer
Nature Customer Service Centre GmbH, Europaplatz 3, 69115 Heidelberg,
Germany. If you have any concerns regarding our products, please
contact ProductSafety@springernature.com

Printed and bound by CPI Group (UK) Ltd, Croydon, CR0 4YY

27/04/2026

02097570-0004